Drama Scripts

~~~~~

Stage

Liz Wainwright

Does Your Mother Dance?

Mixed Company

Elizabeth Wainwright asserts the moral right to be identified as the author of this work. This script is entirely a work of fiction. The names, incidents and characters portrayed in it are entirely the work of the author's imagination. Any resemblance to actual persons living or dead, events or localities is entirely coincidental.
All rights reserved.

No part of this script may be reproduced or transmitted in any form or by any means, electronic or mechanical, including photocopying, recording, or by any information storage and retrieval system without the written permission of the author, except where permitted by law.

Does Your mother Dance
Copyright © Elizabeth Wainwright 2006

Mixed Company
Copyright © Elizabeth Wainwright 1993

Drama Scripts - Stage
Copyright © 2012 Elizabeth Wainwright

Createspace for
Loveday Manor Publishing
www.lizscript.co.uk

ISBN-13: 978-1479304950
ISBN-10: 1479304956

October 2012

To James B.

Wishing you lots of success and good times at the West Yorkshire Playhouse.

CONTENTS

Does Your Mother Dance? 1

Mixed Company 92

Scripts by Liz Wainwright 231

www.lizscript.co.uk

All good wishes,
Liz W.

Liz Wainwright

DOES YOUR MOTHER DANCE?

by

Liz Wainwright

A black comedy with music

Love affairs, family conflicts,

and wanting to be in show business.

CAST

KATHY HYLTON

SUSAN HILTON

JULIE WENTWORTH

PHIL KENDAL

Liz Wainwright

SONGS

I WILL ALWAYS LOVE YOU   (Dolly Parton) - part

IT DOESN'T MATTER ANY MORE   (Buddy Holly)

ALL I HAVE TO DO IS DREAM   (The Everly Brothers)

I'M IN THE MOOD FOR DANCING   (The Nolans)

ALL MY LOVING   (The Beatles)

I WISH YOU LOVE

THE MORE I SEE YOU   (Ballad version, plus upbeat)

ACT I

SCENE 1

The large, elegant but slightly shabby sitting room of an Edwardian house. There are two doors and a French window with red velvet curtains. A red velvet curtain also hangs by the door at one side of the stage and this will be used to represent a theatre.

The room is partly furnished, bookcases, a desk and a couple of dining chairs, a chaise-longue, an ornamental folding screen and a large flat-topped trunk which acts as a coffee table. The only modern thing in the room is a mini hi-fi perched on a foot-stool.

We see the handle of the door jiggling up and down as someone makes a few attempts at opening the door.

KATHY HYLTON *staggers in, carrying a bulging sports bag and a cardboard box containing CDs etc.*

She's an attractive 30- something, ambitious, independent - but also a dreamer. She's come straight from work, so she's wearing a short-sleeved black dress with a tailored black jacket.

During this scene she makes herself more familiar with the room and shows us round it. She also gradually unpacks the contents of the box and the sports bag, arranging things on shelves or piling them up ready to be taken into the bedroom.

KATHY:

My new flat. Do you like it?

She puts down the box and the bag, and walks towards the French windows.

It's the ground floor of the house so I've got some garden and these French windows. There's only one bedroom, *(indicates the other door)* through there - but it's massive.
I've bought a bed. It's a double. I was going to buy a single, but it would have looked daft in a big room like that.

She takes a few books out of the box and later finds space for them on the bookshelves. She also takes out some CDs which she stacks in a pile on the floor next to the hi-fi.

It's going to be a TutTut-free zone this flat. TutTut's my nickname for my mother - ever since I was a teenager. Whatever I did, or said, she'd make this noise *(Tuts)*
Every time I told a joke to make my Dad laugh, he'd laugh but she'd just pull that face of hers and go *(Tuts loudly)*.
No wonder her front teeth stick out a bit. You don't mention her teeth, though, or anything else about her looks, unless you're going to pay her a compliment.

I used to do that, say she looked nice, to try to make her like me a bit more, but it made no difference so I gave up bothering.
She's found a new interest, you know, Susan Hilton, the 'merry widow' - painting her bloody nails!

This house is Edwardian. It's only about half an hour by car from Leeds, and only ten minutes from Gregson's where I work. We do patios and driveways and there's a garden centre as well, so Gregson's got the whole lot covered - on the basis that he gets all the money and I do all the work. Gregson's Gardens - just outside Otley.

You might not have heard of Otley, it's a little market town that's got itself on the tourist map recently. They've got a farmers' market now as well, you know, where you can buy carrots with muck on them. Sorry, am I going on a bit? Andrew says I can talk for England.
Andrew's my boyfriend. We've been living together for years. He thinks I'm round at my friend's house tonight, babysitting.

I've always wanted to live somewhere old, with a bit of history. *(She reclines on the chaise-longue)* And I've always fancied one of these. This isn't my furniture, well, it is now, because I bought it with the flat.

These things used to belong to the old lady who lived here. She was in show business, that's why it's all a bit theatrical. I like that, though. I can be a bit theatrical myself – especially when my lousy boss goes off playing golf instead of signing cheques.

She unzips the sports bag, takes out some tops and cardigans and piles them on the trunk/coffee table.

I'm in show business as well, actually, part-time. I'm a singer. Kathy Hylton – you won't have heard of me. It's the only thing I really want to do, singing.

My Auntie Julie, my Mother's sister, believes everyone should have what they want in life, at least once, even if it's only for a little while. The problem is, she says, choosing the right thing to want.

The estate agent had to get a charity to come in and clear the old lady's stuff – she had no family. It's sad that, isn't it, when you've no children or anybody. All the things that make up your memories, got rid of – and that's your life, gone.

Carefully she takes a pair of silver high-heeled shoes out of the bag.

This is mostly my Dad's stuff I've got here. Not these!
I'll have to make a few more trips to get the rest of my things over here, can't get much in my little car.
You might have gathered, I'm leaving Andrew. I don't know how I'm going to tell my Mother. She thinks the sun only shines when Andrew bends over. She'll demand to know why I'm finishing with him, and I don't know what to tell her. She won't understand – no change there then!

You see, me and Andrew have got on really well most of the time, and let's face it, we've been living the good life. Neither of us wants kids, so we haven't even talked about getting married.

(Sits on the edge of the chaise-longue)

No, I just looked at Andrew one night, sitting there putting his new slippers on and a funny sort of panic swept through me as I suddenly focused on these slippers. They were old man slippers, brown and beige tartan with a tab up the front. His mother bought them for him as part of his Christmas present. My Mother still buys me slippers, she can never think what else to get me.

Anyway, there he was, the 36 year old who lies about his age, the man who works out at the most expensive gym in Leeds in order to maintain the body beautiful, there he was, putting on these old man slippers and liking them.
'They're cosy', he said, 'and they're back in fashion'. Yeah, right!
We had a bit of an argument about it actually. And it made me think, is this it? Is this all there is? Suddenly I could see us ending up like my Mum and Dad, sitting in our separate chairs, with nothing to say to each other.

It wasn't only the slippers. We had this big row about money as well.

Don't get me wrong, Andrew's a nice chap, as men go, and gorgeous to look at. And we've had some great times together, fabulous holidays, New York, Thailand, and Monte Carlo of course, for the Grand Prix. He's car mad is Andrew. That's the only thing TutTut doesn't like about him, the speed he drives at. She's sold my Dad's old car and bought herself a little Toyota.

When my Dad died we found out he had this secret building society account. I reckon it was his 'escape fund'.
He was good with money, my Dad. He looked after the books at the Co-op for years, till they brought in computers and made him redundant.
I went to see him at work once. It must have been really lonely sitting on his own all day in that dark little office of his. I reckoned that's why he smoked, for company.

He left me and my brother, Robert, seven grand each. That's what I used for the deposit on this place. I need Andrew to buy me out of the flat, sorry, 'penthouse apartment', we bought together in Leeds. I've had to get a bank loan as well as a mortgage for this place till the flat's sold. I wasn't going to ask my Mother for any money.

I had to explain all this to Philip Kendal at the bank. He was very understanding. He's about the same age as me, or a bit older. He was quite chatty, divorced – no kids, fortunately, he said. He's been very helpful.

TutTut seems to have really got the hang of spending money, after being tight-fisted for as long as I can remember – as far as I was concerned anyhow.
It's this new friend she's been going out with the last couple of months, Sandra Machin, 'Sandy' she calls herself. Divorced twice and going out with this builder.

Our Robert, he's a builder as well, took my Mother to one of these property advertising parties. She loves free champagne. And she met 'Sandy' who was there with this boyfriend. Sounds daft calling him her 'boyfriend' at her age.

My Mother's 60 next birthday, but you daren't mention it. She was two years younger than my Dad. They should never have got married. It would have been their 30th wedding anniversary this year. Their Silver Wedding celebration was a right farce!

I moved out not long after it. I couldn't wait to leave home, I couldn't stand seeing TutTut upsetting my Dad.

She takes a framed photograph out of the box and places it on the bureau.

My Dad was such a lovely man. His real name was John, but everybody called him Jack, because of some band-leader. My Dad loved music.

She sits on the floor and looks through the pile of CDs.

These are all his Shelley Summer CDs. My Mother didn't want them. You'd think she would, because she and my Dad met at a dance in the sixties, and the first time they danced together, it was to a Shelley Summer record, 'Hey, Baby', her first top twenty hit. (sings)'Hey, hey baby, I wanna know woh woh woh ,)

My Dad wanted to name me after Shelley, or Julie after my Auntie Julie, but he didn't dare. Katherine was my Grandma Rosie's idea, she was a big fan of Katherine Hepburn, and apparently my Mother was past caring so in the end my Dad went and registered me without telling her.

My brother was named after my Mother's father, Robert Benson, so I suppose it was my Dad's turn to pick a name. Kathy Hilton, I've always liked my name.

She takes some photos, theatre programmes and two large scrapbooks out of the box.

My Dad loved Shelley Summer. She was an American singer in the 1960s, she sang a bit of everything, country and western and blues as well as pop. She didn't have a massive amount of big hits – she mostly did cover versions of other people's stuff, but she was very popular and my Dad had a thing about her, thought she was really special.

He kept these big scrap-books with loads of pictures of her and newspaper articles. He was crazy about her, thought she was the best girl singer ever. (*She holds up a framed photo of Shelley Summer*) And the most beautiful of course.

She looked a bit like Marilyn Monroe, or Dolly Parton, with her blonde hair and the way she dressed. And the make-up. She was quite sexy. My Dad never said she looked sexy, though. Sex was never mentioned in our house.

She places the photo next to the hi-fi.

He used to tell me over and over again, when my Mum wasn't there, about seeing Shelley on stage in 1972. They both went that time. Shelley had come over to England for the first time – to meet her Dad.
My Mother didn't go to her other show the following year. My Dad never said why not. Perhaps they couldn't get a babysitter for our Robert, or perhaps they just couldn't afford two tickets.

Every Tuesday, when TutTut went to her Women's Institute meetings, me and my Dad would have a great time looking at Shelley's photos, and playing her CDs and singing along to them. You're probably wondering why I'm going on about all this, and you've probably never heard of Shelley Summer. My friends haven't. They think I'm off my trolley.

You see, I'm working up this tribute act, imitating Shelley Summer.
I do some of my own stuff as well, but it's mainly Shelley - she's still got quite a fan club over here. I started to really try to imitate her for my Dad when he got poorly. Lung cancer. He smoked quite a bit. Who wouldn't, living with my Mother?

She looks in the bag again and pulls out a white fur wrap.

Shelley went for the glamour image later in her career, when she'd started to look a bit silly in mini-skirts. She was one of these women who know how to stay looking good - like my Auntie Julie.
I've gradually collected quite a bit of costume and stuff, and I've even had a wig made professionally. I haven't brought that yet, Andrew might notice if that had gone, it's in a special box in the top of the wardrobe. I'll put it on and show you when I've . .
I know it's a weird thing to do, pretending to be somebody else, but it's . . .
I don't want to be me at the moment, that's for sure. I'm not a nice person. I haven't told Andrew I'm leaving him.

I'm being really sneaky about it, bringing my stuff here bit by bit, because I don't want to have to go back to get things when it gets nasty. And it's bound to get nasty, isn't it?

She takes the scrapbooks and puts them on a bookshelf.

Andrew wants me to give up this Shelley Summer act, he was against it right from the start, really, but he did come with my Dad to my first gig, in a local pub. It was the last time my Dad went anywhere.

You should have seen his face that night. He was thrilled to bits, reckoned I was going to be a star. He was so proud.

Andrew said I was OK, but 'don't give up the day job'.

TutTut had one of her screaming fits when she found out about the act. She told me I had to pack it in, there and then, but my Dad said 'no way'.

She couldn't stop me, but she insisted on me changing the spelling of my name to Hilton with a Y so people wouldn't know we're related. Suits me.

She puts a Dolly Parton CD in the CD player and takes off her jacket.

I bought this mini hi-fi for here. Andrew will want to keep our hi-fi - it's top of the range, like everything else he buys.

She looks in the bag again and pulls out a pink cowboy hat.

Shelley Summer was only a kid of 16 when she left home to go to Nashville. Her Dad had disappeared from her life when she was a little girl. He went away to fight in the war and never came back - by choice.
Her mother, Tina, was like mine, not the forgiving kind. She wouldn't allow Shelley to even speak about him, and Shelley had to spend her life making up for what her Daddy had done.
When the miracle happened and her mother found somebody else willing to marry her, Shelley couldn't get away fast enough. Like my Auntie Julie when she left home, and me.

It was her Dad's best friend, Dean Gilby, who took her to Nashville. She did really well - couldn't have done a darned thing without him of course! That was the way men saw things in those days. And Shelley went along with that, till, the usual story, Dean decided she belonged to him and, you know . . .

She puts the hat on the back of her head as we hear the track 'I Will Always Love You'

```
The Dolly Parton song 'I Will Always Love You'
was one of my Dad's favourites.  He still
loved my Mother, you see, that's what my
Auntie Julie thinks, anyway.
```

KATHY sings along with the CD.

When the track ends she turns off the CD player, and slowly takes off the hat.

```
I'm going to tell Andrew tomorrow.  I'll have
to.
```

Lights down.

A dining chair is placed centre stage to represent SUSAN's dining room.

SCENE 2

KATHY stands quietly in a spotlight.

KATHY:

He was all right about it. Well, not too bad. He was angry when he found out I'd been planning it for weeks, in secret. He didn't deserve to be lied to, he said. I felt awful.

Anyway, we were in the dining room when I broke the news to my Mother – it has a through-lounge my Mum and Dad's semi but she insists on calling it a dining room. I'd gone round for tea, a big mistake as we always had the family rows round the dining table.

SUSAN HILTON *(lilac fingernails and eye-shadow to match, all-shades-of- gold flashed hair and horrendous lilac and gold 'leisure suit') storms on to the stage, gives her daughter a hard shove towards the dining chair and speaks to the audience.*

SUSAN:

I told her!

(To Kathy) You must be out of your tiny mind! Throwing away a chance like that. He'd have asked you to marry him in the end. Katherine, are you listening to me?

(Kathy mimes 'No' to the audience)

SUSAN:

I mean, you've bought that luxury apartment together and he took you to London to meet his parents.

KATHY:

Yeah, great success that was.
Andrew's Mother, who obviously didn't think I looked the part, spent most of the time giving me a list of instructions about how to look after her precious son properly. And all his Dad was interested in was whether he was going to miss his tennis match, so he didn't even stay around to talk to me.

SUSAN:

They were a lovely family.

KATHY:

You never met them.

SUSAN:

You'll never find anybody better than Andrew Sanderson.
I knew that the moment I introduced him to you. You'd never have been invited to that Marks and Spencer's party if it hadn't been for me.

KATHY:

You only took me because my Dad had to stay in bed with that chest infection, and you don't like going anywhere on your own.

SUSAN:

They've made him a manager and they keep sending him on these courses, grooming him, - Andrew's going places.

KATHY:

Yeah, London probably. That's another thing, I don't want to go and live in London. I don't really want to live in a city.

SUSAN:

You're as bad as your father, he'd never move. I'd love one of those luxury city centre apartments.

KATHY:

Overlooking the canal.

SUSAN:

You bought one.

KATHY:

Only because Andrew went on and on saying we had to because it would be a good investment.

SUSAN:

He was right, it's always good to have property.

KATHY:

Oh, yeah. The man, unless it was my Dad, always has to be right – drives me crackers.

SUSAN:

(To the audience) It's a fabulous apartment. Two hundred and fifty thousand pounds.

(To Kathy) Oooh! I hoped and prayed you'd become Mrs Sanderson.

KATHY:

(To the audience) She'd thought at first Andrew's parents might be <u>the</u> Sandersons, the fabric people – she always liked Sanderson curtains. His Dad was actually a big cheese in the pharmaceutical industry – where the real money is. She was very impressed that 'Alistair and Lydia' do nothing but go on cruises now he's retired.

SUSAN:

It's not too late to change your mind.

KATHY:

No, but I'm not going to.

SUSAN:

You're just being stupid and stubborn as usual.

SUSAN strikes a pose.

Andrew's everything a woman could wish for. He's so good looking, and clever, and so classy with it! He's the kind of man you dream about!

KATHY:
You bloody marry him then, if you think he's so flaming marvellous!

For a moment SUSAN stands in the spotlight, obviously considering her chances.

Then she sees KATHY staring at her and looks away as the spotlight fades her out.

KATHY steps forward as the lights come up on her flat again.

SCENE 3

KATHY:

(*to the audience*) Can you believe it? For a minute she wondered what her chances were. She's nearly sixty years old, for God's sake!

She opens the ornamental screen to its full width.

I've got a gig tonight, at the Pink Flamingo in Wakefield. It's a Gay Club. Chesney Barker, my agent - he used to be a comedian on the club circuit - says they'll love it if I sing 'Secret Love'.

I'll have to get ready in a minute. They've no dressing room at this club, only the ladies toilet. You can imagine. So I said I'd get ready at home.

She earned some really big money you know, Shelley. She could get £10,000 a week for a booking at a theatre or a big club. That was fantastic money in those days. I could do a lot with money like that, set up my own business for a start, instead of working for an idiot like Gregson.

Not long after my Dad died my Mother found his Shelley Summer collection, his programmes and scrapbooks and that, and, can you believe it, she was going to throw it all away.

It was a good job I happened to call round to pick up his CDs. I grabbed it all off her and took it round to the flat to keep it safe. I've got Dad's Shelley Summer videos as well. Our Robert managed to get some tapes of her shows, probably bootleg but Robert didn't give a damn, he just wanted to get them for our Dad. He gave them to him for his 50th birthday.

They were never that close, Robert and my Dad. It was me and my Dad, and Mum and Robert.

She takes out a make up mirror and box of make-up. She begins to pin back her hair and apply her Shelley Summer make-up.

I like to get ready in here rather than the bedroom. It's the curtains and everything, gets me in the mood to perform. Brings me luck.

Dad used to say Shelley had a lovely smile, and a sort of sparkle about her. He was right, she had something special when she was singing. Magic, my Dad called it.

She unpacks a pair of shoes and goes behind the screen to change.

It was special time for Shelley when she came to England. She hadn't seen her Dad since she was a little girl.

He married the wrong woman, like my Dad. And during the war he was stationed in Lincolnshire and met Connie, and he couldn't leave her.
He kept writing to Shelley but her Mother didn't let her see his letters. He told Shelley that the Beatles song, 'All my Loving' was special to him, because of her, so she used to include it in her act after they got back together. She loved her Dad like I loved mine.
I'll have to stop all this emotional stuff or I'll be saying goodbye to my mascara. I've been a bit emotional since I left Andrew. Well, you're bound to feel it, aren't you? And being on your own again . . . . Well, it's . . . .
My Mother keeps going on to our Robert about what a big mistake I've made, and apparently Andrew still goes round to see her.
It's nice of him, but I hope it doesn't mean they're plotting for us to get back together.

Andrew can't believe I've left him. He likes to be the one who makes the decisions.

I reckon my Mother's just worried I might want to move back in with her. I don't think she really wanted another child, she was happy just having our Robert, her little boy.

She puts on the wig and steps out from behind the screen, wearing the white dress, puts on the shoes and picks up the white fur stole.

Thank God I had my Dad, and that he had his Shelley Summer.

SCENE 4

Curtain across the set. Spotlights and the sounds of an audience at a show in a nightclub. At one side of the stage is a chair and a small table, with a drink on it.

KATHY sings 'I GUESS IT DOESN'T MATTER ANY MORE' (Buddy Holly} and 'ALL I HAVE TO DO IS DREAM' (The Everly Brothers)

At the end of the songs there is applause, the lights dim a little, the audience sounds fade away. Kathy moves towards the table and eventually sits down to enjoy the drink as SUSAN walks into the club, looking around, horrified.

KATHY:

Andrew and my Mother turned up. I couldn't believe it.

SUSAN:

(to the audience) We planned it as a surprise. I didn't know where to put myself, and poor Andrew, well . . .
It was very good of him to agree to stay until we'd seen Kathy's act. And then she went and sang that Buddy Holly song, you know, the one about 'You go your way and I'll go mine'.

KATHY:

I didn't know Andrew was going to be there.

PHILIP KENDAL, 38, perceptive, fun- loving and doggedly decent, walks on to the stage and speaks to the audience.

PHIL:

What made it worse was that I turned up as well. I was very keen to see Kathy again.

SUSAN:

Aren't you going to introduce me, Katherine?

KATHY:

This is Philip Kendal. My Mother.

PHIL:

Very pleased to meet you, Mrs Hilton. Hope you don't mind my coming, but I'd seen the gig on Kathy's website.

SUSAN:

You've got a website!

KATHY:

My agent got it set up for me - everybody has them these days.

SUSAN:

Have you met Andrew, Katherine's boyfriend? He brought me. He's just . . . Are you a friend of my daughter's, Mr Kendal? She hasn't mentioned you.

PHIL:

I'm her bank manager.

SUSAN:

Oh.

KATHY:

He arranged the mortgage on my new flat.

SUSAN:

I see. Andrew's just gone to . . .I think he's rather upset, Katherine.

KATHY:

Yeah, I could see he was dead uncomfortable being here. All the leather and lipstick's not his sort of thing.

SUSAN:

Well, it's not, very nice.

KATHY:

Typical!

PHIL:

I didn't realise it was a Gay Club either. *(laughs)* I've had a couple of offers!

SUSAN exits. PHIL stays for a moment looking at KATHY. Then he also exits.

SCENE 5

KATHY remains in the spotlight on her own.

KATHY:

TutTut and Andrew didn't stay long afterwards, Andrew took her home. Phil bought me a drink and we had a little chat. He's thinking of having his driveway done and a patio, so I might see him at work. I gave him my extension number.

I told my Auntie Julie about my Mother coming to a gay club. She thought it was hilarious. She and my Mother aren't at all alike. Julie loves music. This is an Abba CD she gave me.

Plays 'Dancing Queen'

Mind you, my Dad reckoned the Benson family only survived because my Mother took over the running of the house and everything.

JULIE WENTWORTH *(nee Benson) shimmies on to the stage, 62, dyed red/gold hair, Julie is glamorous, vivacious, and a little lost. She speaks to the audience.*

JULIE:

Yeah, we'd probably have starved without her. It should have been me, of course, taking charge, looking after everything, I was the eldest - but not reliable, according to Dad.

KATHY:

(to the audience) My auntie Julie has other talents, like making people laugh.

JULIE dances across the stage and twirls KATHY round

JULIE:

And dancing, don't forget the dancing.

They dance together for a while

KATHY:

You always were a great dancer. You even managed to get my Dad on his feet – after a few pints, of course. *(she pauses)* Julie, when did my Mother stop dancing?

JULIE:

I don't know. What makes you ask that?

KATHY:

Phil Kendal, that night at the club, he asked me, 'Does your Mother dance?' She doesn't, does she? But she used to, that's how she met my Dad.

JULIE:

Yeah. She went dancing when she was a teenager – when Old Misery Guts would let her. And when we were little we used to dance together in the front room when your Grandad was at work. Your Grandma Rosie used to join in sometimes, she was a great little mover, our Ma.

She winks at KATHY before draping herself on the chaise longue.

KATHY:

She was a bit of a goer wasn't she!

JULIE:

Yeah, my Dad used to say I took after her – and he didn't mean it as a compliment.

KATHY:

My Mother's like him, isn't she? All 'what will people think' and 'how much is that going to cost?'

JULIE:

Don't be too hard on her, she is the way she is partly because of your Dad's parents. The Hiltons looked down on your Mother and our family – well your Dad's mother, Florence Hilton, did. Grandma Hilton used to be quite nasty to your Mother. Even after they were married she made it very clear that Susan Benson was in no way good enough for her son. He was their only child, you see, and they didn't have him till they were in their forties.

KATHY:

From what I've heard, they were too old and too set in their ways to have children, really.

JULIE:

Yes, your Dad used to say there was no such thing as fun in their house.

KATHY:

There wasn't much in ours either, except when you turned up.

JULIE:

Like a bad penny. It's OK, I know what your Mother used to say. And she was right in some ways. I couldn't wait to get away from her and my Dad and their 'rules'. As soon as I hit 21 I was out of there.

KATHY:

You came back though.

JULIE:

Yeah, for your Mum and Dad's wedding.

KATHY:

And when I was born.

JULIE:

Oh, yes.

JULIE gets up and gives KATHY a kiss before exiting with a wave.

SCENE 6

KATHY:

(to the audience)

I remember Grandma Rosie telling me that Auntie Julie made more fuss of me when I was a baby than my Mother did.
I've always felt there's a special bond between me and my Auntie Julie. She hasn't got any children. She was really pleased when I moved in with Andrew. I stayed on the pill, though. Neither of us wanted kids. I've told Auntie Julie, there's no chance now really.

Julie had a brilliant time in the 60s and 70s. She married a drummer in a pop group and they travelled all over the place till he got into drink and drugs. She divorced him, and had a bit of a drink problem herself for a while.
I was only 10 at the time but I remember her knocking back the sherry at Grandad Benson's funeral.
My Mother never seemed to really get over her Dad dying. And whenever something upset her she used to take it out on me. All through my teens we had nothing but rows. What made it worse was that our Robert could do no wrong.

He could be as selfish as he liked and Mum still thought he was marvellous.

He worked hard, I'll give him that. He started as a bricklayer and now he's got his own company, building flats and converting old houses.

It's all about money with our Robert, though. Just like my Mother. She thinks he's marvellous because he's got a big house, flash car, designer clothes.

He's a tough cookie, our Robert, and he doesn't half like his own way.

I feel sorry for Sharon, his wife, the well-known typing error - the T is next to the R. He has her running round after him, and he hardly does anything to help in the house.

He'd no intention of getting married, hadn't our Robert, enjoyed bachelor life to the full, as they say.

TutTut reckoned Sharon trapped him into marriage - he thought she was on the pill. So it was a quick wedding followed by the arrival of twins. Like Andrew said, giving me one of those 'don't even think about it' looks of his, Robert and Sharon aren't what you'd call a good advert. for family life.

Don't get me wrong, Robert loves his kids.
He's really good at playing with them, like my Dad was.
He and my Dad had some lovely times when he was little. It was only when Robert got money-minded like my mother, and went off the rails when he was a teenager that they didn't have much time for each other.
It broke Robert up when my Dad died. He felt he'd let him down, not going to visit him when he was ill. He couldn't bear to see him like that.
I used to get mad, and tell him he was being selfish as usual, thinking about himself more than what our Dad needed. But then I realised, not everybody can do it.
My Mum could. She looked after my Dad all the time, did everything, but I never saw her . . . She didn't give him cuddles like I did.
She's helped Sharon a lot with the kids. She cuddles them, or rather they cuddle her. She wasn't happy when she first found out she was going to be a grandma - she didn't want people thinking she was that old, silly cow.

But like I say, she's been great with Sharon and the kids. Sharon really appreciates it. I think she's got quite fond of her. She doesn't call her Mum, it's always Susan, but you can understand that, you only have one Mother.

Lights down.

END OF ACT ONE

ACT II

SCENE 1

Lights up on Kathy, wearing jeans and a baggy shirt, pushing a large, heavy old armchair into position – front of stage right.

KATHY:

She's sold the bloody house! She kept that quiet. Even our Robert didn't know. It's our home, that. I was three when we moved in. It's my home.

SUSAN enters.

SUSAN:

It was. You moved out. Couldn't wait, if I remember rightly.

KATHY:

My Dad's not been dead six months and you're selling his house!

SUSAN:

It's my house as well, I've worked hard, just as hard as your Dad. You've never appreciated what I've done all these years, saving up so we could have a lovely home.

KATHY:

Oh, yeah, 'a lovely home'! We hardly dared walk on the bloody carpets or put a cup down anywhere! My Dad used to say you were worse than his mother.

SUSAN:

Don't you talk to me about his mother! She never gave me a minute's peace, that woman, coming round and pulling a face if there was a speck of dust anywhere.

And your Dad might have complained sometimes about me being fussy, but, make no mistake about it, he liked being looked after, having good meals and a nice, clean and tidy house to come home to.

KATHY:

Oh, yeah? If he liked it so much, your house, why did he go down the pub all the time?

SUSAN:

He went there to smoke. And a lot of good that did him! I have to move, there's too many bad memories there for me now.

It took me over, that house, cleaning it and looking after you two and your Dad. None of you were interested in me, you were selfish, all of you. It's time for me now!

She flounces out, slamming the door behind her.

SCENE 2

KATHY:

It was very quiet when she'd gone. The irony is, I'd been quite pleased when she'd told me she was coming round. She'd invited herself, of course, she always does, and you can't really say no, can you? But . . . I like having visitors.

I've had one or two friends round, but it's always a bit awkward, isn't it, when you split up. People are friends with you as a couple, and it's like you're making them choose between you.

She arranges a cushion on the armchair.

She's bought this flat in Ilkley, to be near 'Sandy'. It's a place Sandra's boyfriend has just finished building, very modern and very safe, TutTut said. She's got this thing about being safe.

From what our Robert said, Mother had a great time looking round for somewhere to move to, being nosy about other people's houses. She and 'Sandy' made quite a hobby of it for a while.

Robert told me that she'd looked at some flats in Leeds. She's always liked the idea of living in Leeds, being near all the shops, but Dad would never leave Otley.

Anyway, Leeds was too expensive, so she's bought this flat in Ilkley. She wants to start a new life, she says. What was wrong with the old one?

She lovingly strokes the back of the chair.

I'm not sure she ever really loved my Dad, you know. They never rowed in front of us but once, when they thought I'd gone out, I heard her yelling at my Dad, accusing him of wishing he'd married somebody else instead of her. I didn't hear him denying it.

She curls up in the armchair.

This was my Dad's chair, the only bit of furniture I really wanted from the house. I used to spend hours sitting in this chair on his knee, talking or singing, or him reading me stories when I was little. My Auntie Julie used to sit on Dad's knee as well, just for a bit of fun. You could see TutTut didn't like it.

All the memories there are in this chair. I spent loads of time with my Dad at the end. I'm glad about that. I'd not gone round as much after I moved in with Andrew. You get busy. You know.

Kathy goes over to a shelf and picks up a holiday brochure with a leaflet in it.

Mind you, I'd have gone round a lot more often if TutTut hadn't been there. I wanted to take him out, but every time I did, you had to ask her along as well.
But we had some good times, me and my Dad. And we thought the world of each other. I miss him so much.

She takes out the leaflet.

I feel I'm really making progress with the act, and I've had quite few more bookings, so I'm travelling about a lot. Gregson moans about me taking holiday 'when it's not convenient' but so what?
Chuckling Chesney's got me a really good booking, well, money-wise it is. A week in this club in Ibiza. Nosey Parker saw the leaflet. 'Another 'Gay Place', I suppose.'

I ignored it. She never was interested in anything I achieved, it was never good enough. All she cared about was the bloody house - and now she's gone and sold it!

It's just as well I'm going away - let things calm down a bit. And stop me getting too involved with Phil Kendal.

Exits as PHIL KENDAL walks on stage, wearing glasses, a business suit, and carrying a file.

SCENE 3

PHIL sits at the desk.

PHIL:

I fancied her straight away, as soon as she walked into my office I took my glasses off. I don't need them really but I started wearing them to make people take me more seriously. It was that or a beard, and beards are in the 'undesirables' section of the bank's unwritten rule book. It's a thick book, often written by thick people, but you don't let them know that if you want to fit in. I've always been keen to 'fit in' – comes of being an only child I suppose. I love company.

He looks through the file of papers.

I thought at first Kathy was one of those scary career women, like Fiona, my ex, turned out to be, the way she sat there in her smart suit, and went through her financial situation.
At least she's getting some money out of that flat she bought with Andrew.
Fiona got the biggest share of the equity from our house when we got divorced.

I knew I was being soft, but sometimes there's only so much aggro you can take. To tell the truth, in the end I just wanted rid of her – and her money-minded, stuck up parents. Apparently they'd told Fiona as soon as they met me that they were 'disappointed' in her choice. They found her someone more suitable eventually – unfortunately it was after we'd got married.

He closes the file and walks towards the audience, glasses in his hand.

I gather Kathy had much the same reaction from Andrew's parents. And her mother with her in-laws. Must be a global problem. I felt a bit sorry for Kathy's mother that night at the club, but when I started to talk to Kathy about her I got a very strong 'shut up or I walk' signal.

My parents have retired and gone to live in Spain. I think they've given up any hope of grandchildren. Who can blame them?

Kathy doesn't really want me around at the moment. I'm worried that Andrew is still. . .

I've had to assure her it's more or less a business arrangement - her advising me about re-designing my garden, building a patio etc. She's very talented.

I told her she should be a designer, patios, gardens etc. She could set up her own business. 'Yeah', she said, 'You rob that bank of yours for me, and I'll do it!'

I've managed to get her to come round to my house a couple of times, look at the garden etc and she's let me cook her lunch. She said her Mother would have been impressed with how tidy my house was.
We've been out together for a drink or a meal after a gig - she's always on a high then, happy to have someone to share it with. I think it's brilliant her singing. She's . . . I keep having to play it cool, though, or she'll stop taking my calls.

Lights down.

SCENE 4

Kathy, wearing a long, glitzy dress is on stage at a night club in Ibiza, singing

'I'M IN THE MOOD FOR DANCING' .

She stops singing and faces the audience.

TutTut only followed me to Ibiza! Sandy, who came with her of course, said my Mother wanted to try to make it up with me after the fight over selling the house. She was very upset, Sandy said. She wasn't the only one! And what's it got to do with Sandra Machin?
I nearly died when TutTut came dancing in front of me and waving! She was wearing loads of make-up and gold jewellery and a skimpy red dress with a neckline like Niagara Falls.

KATHY carries on singing and watches in horror as SUSAN dances sexily on to the stage wearing her Ibiza outfit. KATHY finishes the song, walks across and drags her mother off the dance floor.

KATHY:
What are the hell are you doing, here?
SUSAN:
Sandy thought I needed a holiday. And she said you might like a bit of support.

KATHY:

Support! I could hardly sing for embarrassment up there. You should see yourself, jigging about, wiggling your hips and shaking your boobs.

SUSAN:

Don't be crude!

KATHY:

And look at you? What are you doing, Mother, trying to win the mutton dressed as lamb rosette?

SUSAN:

Sandy said I needed cheering up.

KATHY:

How long are you here for?

SUSAN:

Only a week.

KATHY:

Thank God for that!

SUSAN:

Thanks for the welcome! It's a good job we came, by the look of it. Who's that fella who was chatting you up before the show? I didn't like the look of him. You don't want to be getting into one of these holiday romances that end up with you coming home with a souvenir you don't want.

KATHY:

Not that it's any of your business, but he's the guy who owns the club.

SUSAN:

It looked to me as if he's after more than what's in your contract.

KATHY:

Keep your voice down!

SUSAN:

I don't want you getting pregnant before you've got a ring on your finger. You need to be, taking precautions. You know.

KATHY:

It's a bit bloody late to try to tell me the facts of life now. I have been living with Playboy for nearly ten years.

SUSAN:

Do you mean Andrew? I think I'd better go and find Sandy, I didn't like the look of that fella who was buying her a drink. *(exits.)*

SCENE 5

Lights come up on the part of the stage. There's a silk dressing gown on the back of a chair. KATHY picks it up and puts it on over her dress.

KATHY:

I had a show in Watford last week. I went to stay with my Auntie Julie. She's got this really nice flat in London, she bought it when she came home after her husband died. Her second husband - the good one, an American called Bill Wentworth.

He was a bit older than Julie. My Mother used to refer to him as 'Julie's 'Sugar Daddy' because Bill wasn't short of a dollar or two. Dead jealous, she was.

Julie travelled all over the world with Bill, but when he died a few years ago she came back home for good. When I say home, I don't mean our house.

SCENE 6

JULIE sits on the chaise longue and reads a magazine.

KATHY:

(to Julie)

I don't remember my Mother ever really making you feel at home when you came to see us.

JULIE:
Your Dad made up for her. And anyway, London was where I wanted to be. Plenty of life in London. I used to love spending time with you, though, taking you shopping - and dancing! Still do!

KATHY:
I used to wish I was your daughter instead of my Mother's. You wouldn't have come to Ibiza and started telling me how to behave. Ironic, though, wasn't it - in view of what she doesn't know. Our little secret.

JULIE:
Yes.

KATHY:

(to the audience)

Julie came to stay for a fortnight once, when my Mum and Dad went away on holiday without me for the first time. When they were 'old enough to go on their own', as my Dad used to say.

Our Robert was away as well, his 21st birthday holiday trip, and my Mother didn't trust me to be in the house on my own, 'never knew what I'd get up to' she said. She meant boys. It was a bit late for her to worry about that, if only she'd known.

KATHY:

(to Julie)

I remember you were so pleased to be asked that TutTut ended up thinking she was doing you a favour instead of the other way round.

JULIE:

Well we used to have really good laugh, just the two of us.

KATHY:

It wasn't much fun for you that time.

JULIE:

No.

KATHY:

(to the audience)

I'd gone and got myself pregnant you see. There was this lad at school, he was gorgeous,

all the girls fancied the pants off him. They were all jealous when he came after me at that party. *(Beat)* It wasn't very nice. I felt sick afterwards. And then I found out I was pregnant. I was petrified. My Mother would kill me, and my Dad . . .
I didn't want that baby. I tried all sorts, but . . . .
I wished it away in the end. I prayed and prayed that . .
And I got what I asked for, I had a miscarriage.

Julie stands and holds Kathy.

KATHY:

Auntie Julie got the doctor and when he'd gone she gave me a cuddle, and we had a good cry together. We've been even closer since then. She was the only one who knew, it was our secret, and she's never told anybody.
The doctor said I'd have problems having children. I don't deserve to have kids after that, anyway, do I?

JULIE:

Hush, don't say that.

KATHY:

It's great to be able to talk to you. I've got a couple more bookings coming up in London so we can spend more time together.

JULIE:

Ooh, shopping. I'll have no money left!

KATHY:

At least you know how to enjoy it. TutTut seems to give herself a guilt trip every time she buys something.

JULIE:

Perhaps she hears our Dad shouting at her.

KATHY:

No, it's her, she has a way of always seeing the negative side.

JULIE:

I think she is trying to change.

KATHY:

Only when it suits her. She's never realised that you're supposed to enjoy life. I told her the other day – and it didn't go down well – that you don't know how long you've got, so make the most of it.

JULIE:

Yeah.

The lights go down, Julie exits and KATHY takes off her silk dressing gown. She steps into a spotlight and speaks to the audience.

(A small wooden bench is placed at the opposite side of the stage)

KATHY:

```
I've been working on a new song, a ballad
version Shelley did of 'The More I See You'.
It was one of Bill and Julie's favourites.
```

KATHY sings 'THE MORE I SEE YOU' and as she finishes the song and exits, PHIL walks on to the stage and stands by the bench. He's wearing his 'smart casual' clothes and carrying a pink azalea in a basket.

SCENE 7

PHIL:

I like that song. Good words. I met Kathy off the train when she came back from London. She came skipping along the platform all excited like a little girl.

He puts the azalea on the bench and holds out his arms.

She gave me a big hug and a kiss and couldn't wait to tell me her news.

On the train on the way back from her Auntie Julie's she got chatted up by this old fella, well, I don't think he can have been that old. She said she tried to ignore him at first, but it turned out he was OK. He was a television producer, working on a 'Stars in Their Eyes' type show called 'The Big Time'.

Apparently he'd seen the box with her wig in it, the maker's label is on the side, and he asked her about her act.

She must have made a helluva an impression on him because he offered her an audition.

This show, 'The Big Time' is putting tribute acts like hers against new people, the old stars against the new - that's the idea. They're desperate for new angles on these sort of talents shows, aren't they?

He sits on the bench.

We went for a meal and she told me all about it. Some of it's going to be filmed in big old theatres – just to make it that bit different, and to give the theatres a bit of refurbishment revenue. The Final will be a Christmas Special filmed at the London Palladium. She'd love to get to the final and invite Julie as her special guest. She said Julie would love that, seeing her on stage at The London Palladium. So would I.
I was glad it was just Julie she was going to see in London.
Andrew moved there a few weeks ago, big promotion. He's got a flat and made sure Kathy had his address and his home phone number as well as his mobile. I'm pretty sure it's well and truly over between them, but, when you've lived with someone, it takes a while to realise you're never going to be together like that again.
I'm beginning to think I'm in with a chance of a really serious relationship. That's what I want. But Kathy. .
For the audition she sang the Beatles song 'All My Loving' because of the connection with

the story of Shelley Summer coming over to meet her Dad.

They love a good story like that on these shows, apparently. I think the producer gave her a bit of advice on the choice of numbers, but she does love that one and its connections.

PHIL picks up the azalea and walks towards the far side of the stage.

She's got through to the Quarter Final. It's being held at the Grand Theatre in Leeds. Kathy thinks it will be lucky for her because that's where her Dad saw Shelley for the first time.

It was going to be a bit crowded backstage with all the other contestants so she's told them she'd prefer to get ready at home. She knows what she wants, my little Kathy – she'd go mad if she heard me calling her that. You may have gathered I'm not finding this easy! They're sending a car for her. She's hoping for a limo! And so is her mother.

Kathy's really annoyed because her Mother, and 'Sandy' of course, have been all over her since she got on television.

Her brother, Robert and his wife will be there, too and almost everyone she works with, including Gregson.

I've met him a couple of times. I wasn't impressed. I've met workplace bullies like him before and I don't like them. I've developed strategies to deal with them, though. I know I look like a softie but - you'd be surprised. I quite surprise myself sometimes.

Kathy says that Gregson's been in a really dark and aggressive mood these last couple of weeks. Apparently his wife's run off with the steward from the golf club. He thinks everybody's laughing at him - which they probably are, when he's not there.

He's been quite nasty. He shouldn't be taking it out on his employees but, that's the sort of person he is.

Kathy's trying to ignore him. She wants to concentrate on the Shelley Summer act and her own singing. She's beginning to think she could do it full time one day, and earn good money like Shelley Summer did, tour America even. . . .

To be honest, I'm not enthusiastic about the touring aspect. Selfish, I suppose, but she'd be away even more than she is now. You should see have seen her face, though, when she told me about her dream.
'Imagine that', she said, 'earning your living doing something that makes you happy.'
And that's what I want, truly. I want Kathy to be happy.
But with me.

ACT III

SCENE 1

KATHY has bought cushions for the chaise longue and a luxurious throw for the armchair. There's also a hi-fi unit on which stand her mini hi-fi and a large framed photograph of her Dad.

Kathy is dressed for the show – wearing a full-length silver sparkly dress.

There's a large basket of flowers on the desk, Philip's azalea and a pile of 'Good Luck' cards on the chest. During the scene Kathy, nervous, ready too early, arranges the cards round the room.

KATHY:

I've had all these Good Luck cards, and loads of people are coming to support me. Auntie Julie's come up from London.

I was mad about my Mother showing off and pushing me to get more tickets, but Phil said it's good that the family are making a fuss of me, that's what families are for.

He thinks my Mother's hilarious. He says he feels sorry for her as well sometimes. I told him not to bother.

It's great that the Quarter Final is sort of on home ground for me, and that there's the connection with Shelley and my Dad, and her Dad of course.

Shelley's Dad was upset when he found out what had happened between Shelley and her manager, Dean Gilby.
Dean had been her Dad's best friend as a teenager, and she'd trusted him to look after her and help her with her singing career. It ended up the usual story, though, Dean wanting to be in control of everything she did, and wanting more from her than she wanted to give. She had to make a run for it one night to get away from him. She went to New York and her career really started to take off then. She did right. You can't have somebody telling you what to do, what to think.

I realise now it was getting that way with Andrew. I didn't notice it happening, it sort of crept up on me, starting with him deciding what wine we'd buy, what I'd cook for him to eat.
I've enjoyed being able to please myself since I left Andrew, eat what I want, go to bed when I want.
I'm still seeing Phil now and then. Just as a friend. Well, he's not easy to get rid of.

He keeps being so nice, and so reasonable about everything.

I have made it very clear that I don't want anyone taking over my life, or making it more complicated than it needs to be. He just smiles and gives me a kiss.

She picks up the azalea, looking for a better place to put it.

Phil bought me this azalea, and some champagne, to congratulate me. He's been helping me with the business side, and dealing with bookings. I've had loads of people ringing up since I was on tele. Chesney has had to retire - doctor's orders. He'll be there tonight, though, to have his moment. I've got to finish with Phil. He's decided he loves me.

I never wanted it to get serious. This is my big chance. It's important to me. Like I told him before, I can't afford any distractions.

I'll be able to sing for ever if I win this competition - and it's the only thing that makes me really happy - to be up on a stage, singing.

```
That's what Shelley Summer used to say, how
special it was to be in front of an audience,
how they make you feel loved.
```

She places the azalea next to her Dad's photograph.

```
Shelley's Dad was very special to her, like my
Dad was to me.  I'm singing 'All my Loving'
tonight.
```

Lights down.

SCENE 2

Set blacked out.   A spotlight on the curtain and applause represent The Grand Theatre.

Kathy sings **'ALL MY LOVING'.**   *Lights down.*

SCENE 3

Kathy in the flat, sitting on her Dad's chair, wearing the silk dressing gown.

KATHY:

I'm in the Semi-Final, in Blackpool. It's wonderful, but it's a bit scary. My Mother's driving me mad, fussing about and trying to tell me what to do. Talk about over-excited. She'd be even more neurotic about this competition if she knew I'd lost my job.

Gregson said I'd been taking too much time off because of the TV show, and he had a business to run. He was right, but that wasn't the reason I got the push.

When Gregson saw me at the Quarter Final he got ideas. He didn't realise I was sexy, he says, and makes a grab at me in the back room. I shoved my knee where he keeps his brains and he told me to 'clear my desk'. He'd heard that 'clear your desk' is what they say in big business. He'll always be small time, him. Especially now I've gone. I've got to make a go of this now, though.

It's been bad news week. My Auntie Julie said
she wouldn't be able to come to Blackpool.
She wouldn't tell me why, so I knew there was
something wrong and went down to see her.
She's got cancer.
She doesn't want anybody to know and she's
made me promise to keep it secret, like she's
kept that secret for me all these years.
She's decided not to have treatment, there's
no chance anyway really, so why ruin a good
hair-style, she says.

She'll tell my Mother eventually because
there's things they've got to talk about,
things Auntie Julie has to make her
understand.
My Mother hardly said two words to her at my
Dad's funeral. She knows that I keep in touch
with my auntie Julie, but she doesn't like it.
Jealousy again.
Me and Julie had a bit of a cry about the
cancer, but then she insisted we talk about
something more entertaining. Life is for
living, every minute of it, she says, and
making sure you have good memories. She
wanted to hear more about Phil. She wants me

to give him a chance, because 'he might be the one to have babies with.'

'Shut up', I said, 'he's nothing like what I want. He works in a bank, for god's sake – and he tidies up!'

I can really talk to Auntie Julie – so different to my Mother. Mind you, that's not surprising. You know I mentioned my Mum and Dad's Silver Wedding.

Well, Julie and I had a laugh about that as well last week. Though it's nothing to laugh about in a way.

Julie brought Bill to the Silver Wedding Party. They hadn't been married long and she'd been looking forward to introducing him to the family, to show them she'd got something right for once.

Grandma Rosie had been at the Barley Wine, and she was well away. She started flirting with Bill - talk about seventy and shameless! She has a real dirty mind when she's drunk.

My Mother tried to shut her up, but she shoved her away and took Julie to one side.

'I like this fella,' she whispers so that we can all hear her. 'He's an American. I've always liked Americans. Your Father was an American.'

Well, that bombshell took the edge off the Silver Wedding celebrations I can tell you.

But I think Julie was quite relieved in a way, it explained a lot about how her Dad, who wasn't her Dad, had been with her. He must have known, though nothing was ever said. It makes for trouble, sometimes, doesn't it, not talking about things, and keeping secrets.

(Lights down).

SCENE 4

Kathy, in costume apart from the wig, which is in its box beside her, sits on a chair at one side of the stage, lit as if in a theatre dressing room. Her silk dressing gown is on the back of the chair.

The chaise longue is at the unlit side of the stage covered with a hotel bedroom bedspread. SUSAN sits on the edge of it, with a glass and a bottle of champagne.

KATHY:

`(to the audience)` It was last night. What a time to choose, the night before the Semi-Final. TutTut's sitting there, uninvited, of course, in my hotel bedroom, knocking back the free champagne, and she's asking me, again, what I was going to sing.
I'd refused to tell her before because she always has to push her ideas about what I should be doing, what I should be wearing.

She puts on the silk dressing gown and carries the chair across to where SUSAN is sitting, pausing halfway to speak to the audience.

KATHY:

Anyway, I gave in and told her. 'I Wish You Love', because it's a lovely number, and 'The More I See You', because it's my Auntie Julie's favourite. That did it.

Lights come up on Susan.

SUSAN:

Her favourite? Why aren't you singing mine?

KATHY:

Well, I know it's 'My Way' for a start, and I don't like it, and why the hell should I sing your favourite?

SUSAN:

Because I'm your Mother, that's why! Sandy was sure you'd choose something special for me. What am I going to tell her?

KATHY:

Tell her what you like! Who gives a shit what Sandra Machin thinks?

SUSAN:

I do. And don't use that kind of language! It's always been the same, Katherine. You've always thought more of Julie than me – just like your Dad! You're singing a song for her tomorrow night, and she can't even be bothered to come and support you!

KATHY:

She'd come if she could. She's always been there for me as Auntie Julie, more than you'll ever know.

SUSAN:

If she really cared about you, she wouldn't miss seeing you in the Semi Final.

KATHY:

She does care. She loves me more than you've ever done!

SUSAN:

Does she! Then why isn't she here?

KATHY:

Because she's . . . I can't tell you. Right?

SUSAN:

Right. I didn't come here to argue.

She looks at the dress hanging up in front of the wardrobe.

Is that the dress for tomorrow night?

KATHY:

What if it is?

SUSAN:

You can't wear that, it'll show all you've got! You're just like Julie, flaunting yourself! You'll look like a, a flaming barmaid! If you wear that dress I'll never speak to you again.

KATHY:

Good!

SUSAN:

I mean it! I'll disown you. You'll be no daughter of mine!

KATHY:

I wish I bloody wasn't!

SUSAN:

Oh. Do you! Well, you shouldn't have been! She should have been having his child, not me! You should have been hers, not mine, you've even got blonde hair like she had.

SUSAN sinks down on to the bed in tears.

Kathy turns to the audience.

KATHY:

I thought she meant Auntie Julie? But she's always had red hair, not blonde.

Pause.

My Dad had an affair. When my Mother was expecting me. It had been going on for some time. They'd met at that first Shelley Summer show, and after that he'd gone to the pub where she worked – only job she could get in the evenings. She was married, and she had children, too. That's why they stopped seeing each other.

But it was too late, my Mother had found out. My Dad was no good at telling lies, it wasn't in his nature. He cried and said he loved this woman. Marion her name was.

They'd kept it secret, my Mum and Dad, all those years. They'd told nobody. They'd just kept it between them, this terrible thing, between them.

That night, in that hotel room, sitting there on the edge of the bed, like a little child, my Mother talked about it for the first time. And she cried, sobbed her heart out. The first time I'd seen her cry since her Dad died.

SUSAN:
I'd tried so hard to please him. I gave your Dad everything I could, did anything to make him happy. And he still let me down, went off with . . ., he still never loved me.
He even tried to justify what he'd done. And do you know what he said, who he blamed? His mother. And me. The way I was. *(She stands.)*

He said I was disappointed in him, just like his mother was disappointed with his Dad.
His mother hadn't shown him any real love and affection and neither had I.
He said he hadn't known what it was to be kissed and cuddled and to really make love, till he met her, that damned woman. She loved him, he said, in a way nobody else had ever loved him, or ever would.
He hurt me! He hurt me so much! The man you worshipped as your wonderful, perfect father. He hurt me. And I didn't deserve it!

She exits. KATHY sits down and stays there for a while, head bowed.

Then she looks up at the audience again.

KATHY:
Good timing, wasn't it? The night before the semi-final.
I bloody went to pieces. She's sitting there bawling, then I'm sitting there bawling.
Phil reckoned we were both crying for my Dad. Grieving. I phoned him after she'd gone. I had to have somebody to talk to, to hold me — I was falling apart.

```
He came round to my room, made me a cup of
tea.   That's the sort of man he is.
```

PHIL enters and takes KATHY in his arms. They kiss and become increasingly passionate. They move on to the bed.

Lights down.

SCENE 5

KATHY is again sitting in the theatre dressing room. She speaks to the audience.

KATHY:

We . . . You know. Well, I was upset. It was what I needed. And, well, it was bound to happen, sometime, this is the 21st century. It won't happen again, though. I've told him that already. Like I've said, he's not my type.

She picks up the wig box and begins to comb the wig a little with her fingers.

It was bloody good, though. I'll give him that. Fantastic, actually. I've never made love like that before. Such a powerful feeling – it, just took me over.
But that's exactly what I don't want, taking over. He's not what I want.

PHIL enters.

PHIL:

Aren't I, Kathy?   Are you sure?

KATHY:

Yeah. Thanks for last night.

PHIL:

Thanks!

KATHY:

I'm OK now.

PHIL:

Have you seen your Mother?

KATHY:

No.

PHIL:

I think you should.

KATHY:

Do you? You still haven't got the message, have you, Phil?

I don't want anybody giving me advice, telling me what I should be doing.

PHIL:

I'm not.

KATHY:

You are. And it has nothing to do with you. And I don't want even to think about my Mother at the moment. I just want to go on that stage and sing. And I'll be doing it for my Dad.

PHIL:

I know.

KATHY:

I loved him even if she didn't. One mistake. Could she not have forgiven him for just one mistake?

PHIL:

I think you're wrong, Kathy. I think your Mother did love your Dad.

KATHY:

What the bloody hell do you know about it? You don't know my family and you don't know me. And you're not going to. I don't want a man in my life, trying to take it over.

PHIL:

I'm not.

KATHY:

You're not listening to me! Why can't men bloody listen?

I don't want you. I don't want to be with you. I don't want you here. I don't want you in my life.

PHIL stares at her for a moment, then walks out.

Kathy stands and stares after him for a few moments, then turns to the audience.

KATHY:

And that was it, him and me, finished. I don't know if he'll even stay for the show. I hope he does. I did need to break up with him though, for good. I just wish it hadn't been like that.

But I have made the right decision. No relationship is better than what I feel between me and the audience.

Lights down.

SCENE 6

KATHY puts on the wig, and steps forward into a centre stage spotlight and the sound of applause.

She sings ***'I WISH YOU LOVE'.'***

Lights down.

SCENE 7

PHIL wanders aimlessly across the stag, pauses to kick something and turns to the audience.

PHIL:

You can love somebody, you know, even if they don't love you. I stayed to see the show. And so did Susan. She held my hand - crushed it to death actually.

We both cried. I was always taught that as a bloke, you're not supposed to but they even do it on the tele now.

The audience loved Kathy. And she loves them, loves being up there, having what she wants. I can't compete with that. Life's hard work sometimes, isn't it?

SCENE 8

Kathy, in the flat again, wears a full length skirt and a baggy sweater.

She stands looking out of the French window, then turns to the audience.

KATHY:

It was as well I finished with him. He's got transferred to Blackpool, I wouldn't have wanted to move. He wrote me a note after the show, saying it was a terrific performance, and that, if I want to, I can call in and see him when I get top billing at Blackpool Winter Gardens like Shelley did.

She moves forward, pauses by the hi-fi unit, looks at her Dad's photograph, and removes a couple of dead leaves from the azalea next to it.

I'm pregnant.
I can't believe it. I didn't think I'd ever have a child. Not after that miscarriage and what the doctor said, I didn't think I could have kids. Didn't want them either.

My mistake was giving up the Pill after I left Andrew. But it's not good for you to take it for too long, and I wasn't intending to go to bed with anyone.

I don't know what to do, to be quite honest. I don't think I want to have a baby. And you should really want a child, not just have it accidentally like this. What a bloody thing to happen. It's not what I want, not now, when I've got this Shelley Summer thing going so well.

She got pregnant, you know, when she was 16. Her mother forced her to get rid of it.

I haven't told anybody about the baby but I have been to see a doctor to get it confirmed, I don't trust these testing kits. He asked me about my previous medical history, so I had to tell him about the miscarriage.

He says I need to have complete rest or I could lose it. They always say that, though, don't they?

How can I rest? I've got 'The Big Time' Final next week.

And I've a bloody good chance of winning – everybody says so. It's the London Palladium, you only get a chance like this once in your life.

I've told my Mother and Phil that I don't want them there. I don't want them putting me off, I've got to be able to concentrate. I've got to win this - for my Dad, and for me.

I'm going to sing an Everly Brothers hit that Shelley covered. It's called 'All I Have to Do Is Dream'. It was my Dad's favourite, so I've been saving it for the Final.
And I'm singing 'The More I See You', a combination of the ballad version and the upbeat one. That's for Auntie Julie.
She places her hands gently on her stomach)   And this. It'll just have to take its chances.

The lights go down and the curtain closes in front of the set as she exits.

SCENE 9

*We hear the sound of a theatre audience, hear them applauding and then Kathy singing **'ALL I HAVE TO DO IS DREAM'**.*

She appears in a spotlight, in full Shelley Summer costume, still singing as the lights change, but she doesn't complete the song.

She takes off the white fur wrap and folds it in her arms.

KATHY:

I couldn't do it. My Dad wouldn't let me. I wouldn't let me. And Auntie Julie used to say it was her one big regret, that she'd never had children. I'll call it Julie if it's a girl.

I'll tell Phil some time. I'll have to, it's only right. But it's the baby I'm having, not him.

I'm hoping it's a boy, then I can call him Jack. My Dad won't be here to play with him, though, will he? And neither will Auntie Julie.

I'm travelling back down to London next week – for her funeral. She'll be glad I'm keeping the baby.

```
I don't know what happened, something just
took over, and I couldn't. . It won't be easy,
but we'll manage, eh kid?
```

Holding the folded wrap like a baby, she sings **'THE MORE I SEE YOU'**

SCENE 10

Kathy is in the flat, wearing her Shelley Summer costume.

KATHY:

My Mother went down and looked after Julie – just like she looked after my Dad.

I'm having to give up the act – just thought I'd put this on, pretend for a little while that I've won the Final.

No regrets, though.

My Mum's thrilled to bits about the baby – well she's pleased. She'd be thrilled if I was going to marry the father.

It is a boy, by the way, I had the test. So he'll be Jack Hylton – with a Y.

I'll take him to see Phil. The baby will need to know who his Dad is, and Phil will take it seriously, fatherhood. He'll make sure little Jack opens a bank account – that sort of thing.

No, he'll be around, it's only right. The trouble is, I've got a feeling he's going to be delighted. I can just see them both in Blackpool, building sandcastles.

But I'll sort it all out for myself, on my own. I'm not the sort to trap a man into marriage

And, I won't be coping entirely on my own. I have to be practical. I'll be a good mother, though, the best. I'll make sure he's happy, and that he knows he's loved - every day, all his life.

My Mum says she'll look after him while I'm at work. I got my job back - threatened Gregson with a claim for unfair dismissal on grounds of sexual harassment.

And Auntie Julie's left me nearly all her money. It means I can go to college part-time and start my own business eventually, like Phil said I should.

She folds the fur wrap and puts it in a bag, with the end of it still visible.

My Mother's never going to change, not at her age. But at least I understand a bit more why she is like she is. And when I thought about what TutTut had said, when she was ranting on about what her life had been like, I realised we did take her for granted sometimes.

I do remember we'd sit down to meals she'd spent hours cooking, and we'd just eat it and say nothing except,
'Is there any more gravy?'

Pause.

She's forgiven my Dad - now it's too late.
She'll just have to live with that.
She did love him - we've got that in common at least.
That and 'Sleepless in Seattle'. We both love that film. We sat and watched it together the other night - fighting over the box of tissues.

I don't mind giving up the Shelley Summer act - I worked out it was my way of holding on to my Dad.
And I'll still hold on to him, in all sorts of ways. I'll sing Shelley Summer songs to the baby, just the way my Dad used to sing them to me when I was little.
I know what I want out of life now. What I really want.
TuTut's not happy of course.

SUSAN walks on to the stage and talks to the audience.

SUSAN:

I do wish she wouldn't call me that.

She takes the wrap out of the bag and tries it on as she turns to talk to Kathy.

SUSAN:

I really don't think you should give up the act completely, Katherine, not now when you could make good money at it.
It needs changing a bit, though.

KATHY:

Oh, yes?

SUSAN:

Yes. I think you should always close with 'Make Someone Happy'. You know, from the film. The audience would love that, they'd even join in, you know, a bit of a sing-song. Always goes down well that. Katherine, are you listening to me? Katherine!'

KATHY:

No, Mother.

She looks at the audience, shakes her head and exits. SUSAN follows her.

SUSAN:

Katherine! Kathy!

Lights down. Then lights come up as PHIL leads JULIE on to take a bow and dance together to the ballad version of 'THE MORE I SEE YOU'.

JULIE dances to the side and holds out her hand to bring on SUSAN. The two sisters dance together before SUSAN steps forward.

PHIL moves to the other side of the stage and leads on KATHY. They dance closely together before he leads her forward.

The music changes to the upbeat version of the song, and all dance and take final applause.

THE END

MIXED COMPANY

by

Liz Wainwright

Cast

Viv Hoyland

Ellie Marshall

Gwen Courtney

PROLOGUE

Curtain up on an elegant lounge in the 1990s.

A large patio window looking out on to a garden.

A staircase. A deep pink velvet sofa etc, display cabinet, coffee table, drinks cabinet and a writing bureau.

Smaller items include a silver cigarette box and lighter, gold snuff box and a collection of china ornaments. On the bureau is the figurine of an Edwardian lady.

(We expect a 'drawing room play' - but this isn't one)

The room is fastidiously neat and tidy, and lifeless.

As the lights go down a late-comer, **VIV HOYLAND**, *enters the auditorium. VIV is in her 50s, with hacked hair, no make-up, and wears a shabby raincoat.*

Her comfortable, motherly looks and warm, outgoing manner distract you from the cold determination in her eyes.

She stands looking towards the set, a ticket in her hand, and talks to the audience.

VIV:

Bloody hell, look at that!
Have you been here before, because I haven't.
But they were giving away these free tickets,
so I thought, well, why shouldn't I?
I was supposed to come with my friend, Ellie,
but she chickened out because she didn't know
what to wear. Frightened to death in case
people stare at her. It doesn't bother me.

(she steps up on to the side of the stage)

They can stare as much as they bloody well
like!
This is nice, isn't it? Something to look at
if it gets boring, anyway. Like those
Edwardian things on tele - you can always look
at the furniture and that if you get fed up
with them not getting on with it. Do they let
you go round the back?
Well, they can only chuck me out, can't they?
See you later.

She crosses the stage and exits.

The lights fade and then come up again.

ACT ONE

SCENE ONE

*We hear **GWEN COURTNEY** off stage.*

GWEN:

No, I won't forget. Goodbye. (*a car door slams*) Paul, aren't you going to say . ? (*the car drives off*) Goodbye.

We hear the car speeding away. A garage door is closed.

GWEN enters. She's in her 50s, her hair and clothes are immaculate - she wears a navy skirt, white blouse and royal blue cardigan. She's as elegant, and lifeless, as the room.

She tidies a couple of glossy magazines into a rack, and looks round for something else to do.

She exits, returns with a clean yellow duster, and begins to dust ornaments.

Gradually GWEN slows down, aware of the silence, and becoming a little edgy as she hears a sound outside.

She looks out of the window, but then feels she is being foolish and begins to dust again.

She picks up the china figure of the Edwardian lady. She dusts it thoughtfully, puts it down and then stares at the empty space next to it.

She opens a drawer and slowly takes out a graduation photograph of her son. She strokes his face with the edge of the duster.

GWEN:
Hello, young man. Are you all right? Me? Oh, yes, I'm all right. I'm still here, anyway. (*looks at the china figure*) And so is she.

She hugs the photo for a moment and then places it in its rightful place on the bureau.

She looks round the room, aware of the silence.

She's startled when she hears birds scrabbling in the chimney. We hear them squawk and fly off.

Gwen stands very still, uncomfortable in the silence again and wondering what to do next. She turns on the radio – 'Start the Week' chatters.

She re-tunes to Terry Wogan on Radio 2. Nat King Cole's – 'These Foolish Things'. The music takes hold of her, she begins to move like a dancer from a thirties musical, and then sings softly.

Towards the end of the track , VIV silently appears in the doorway.

VIV is now wearing a rain hat, and a shabby, wet coat over a skirt and sweater and baggy cardigan. She carries a shopping bag.

VIV stands very still, watching GWEN carefully, with shrewd, resentful eyes.

When the record ends, GWEN catches sight of herself in a mirror, draws her fingers down her cheeks, and stares pensively at her reflection.

She suddenly becomes aware of VIV watching her.

VIV walks in and switches off the radio.

VIV:
I knocked, but you didn't hear me. You left the back door open.

Seeing GWEN's panic, VIV produces her winning smile.

VIV:
You should keep your door locked, you know.

GWEN:
Yes. Yes, I usually do. I opened it to feed the birds. Who are you?

VIV:
Viv. Viv Hoyland. I'm sorry if I frightened you. I've just come to ask if you know where there's a café round here?

GWEN:
No. No, I'm sorry. I don't.

VIV:
Oh, heck. It's freezing today, isn't it?

GWEN:
I don't know. I haven't really been out yet.

VIV:

I've been out on the streets since eight o'clock. Sometimes you can catch people before they go to work. *(shows a card)* Carpet cleaning service. We're very reasonable. Have you got any you want doing?

GWEN:

No. No, they're all fairly new.

VIV:

Oh. Lucky you, eh?

GWEN:

Yes. Well . . .

She begins to walk towards the door, to show VIV out.

VIV:

It's gonna chuck it down again in a minute.

GWEN:

Oh.

VIV:

Pity there's no caf. I don't suppose you could . . . . just a quick cuppa, warm us up a bit?

Gwen hesitates.

VIV:
It'd be really kind of you. Not a lot of kindness about these days. Go on, just a cup of tea.

GWEN:
Well . . . All right.

VIV:
Oh, thanks very much. I'll just get my mate.

GWEN:
Mate?

VIV exits quickly.

GWEN:
Oh!

GWEN glances round the room, picks up the silver cigarette lighter and the gold snuff box and hurriedly puts them away in a drawer.

VIV enters in time to see this, and looks at GWEN, who feels a little ashamed of her action.

ELLIE MARSHALL *follows VIV, very hesitantly.*

ELLIE is in her early fifties but hates to admit it. Smaller and slimmer than VIV, she wears quite a bit of make-up, including blue eye-shadow, and her blonde rinsed hair is carefully curled.

ELLIE adopts what she thinks is a 'genteel' tone.

ELLIE:
Hello. This is very kind of you.

VIV:

My friend, Ellie. Ellie, this is Gwen.

GWEN:

How do you know my name?

VIV:

Mind if we take our coats off? They're a bit wet.

GWEN:

Oh. Yes. I'll hang them up to dry.

Gingerly GWEN takes the coat and hat VIV thrusts at her.

ELLIE takes off her raincoat and, acutely aware of its shabbiness,- folds it carefully to hide a stain before handing it to GWEN.

ELLIE:

It needs cleaning really, but I thought it'd be best to wait till we'd finished this job. You'd be amazed how dirty some people's front doors are. Not yours, of course.

VIV:

(annoyed at ELLIE's simpering) All right if we sit down?

GWEN:

Oh, sorry. Of course.

VIV makes herself comfortable in an armchair by the fire, but ELLIE hesitates to sit down.

ELLIE:

Viv said you left the door open. You shouldn't do that.

GWEN:

I know.

ELLIE:

It's terrible, isn't it - having to keep your doors locked? But you never know, do you?

GWEN:

No.

VIV smiles slowly. GWEN notices. The two intruders wait expectantly.

GWEN:

I'll make the tea.

ELLIE:

Oh, lovely!

VIV:

I prefer coffee - if you don't mind.

GWEN:

Coffee. Yes.

VIV:

But Ellie likes tea.

GWEN nods and goes towards the door, glancing at the silver cigarette box as she leaves.

VIV sees this and they look at each other for a moment, before GWEN looks away and hurries out. VIV warms herself at the gas fire, and leans forward to turn it up.

ELLIE:
Viv!

VIV:
I'm cold.

ELLIE seems almost unable to take in her surroundings at first and just stands and stares at everything.

ELLIE:
Isn't it fabulous!

VIV:
It's warmer in here than it is out there, I know that!

ELLIE:
I hope Jacko doesn't catch up with us.

VIV:
He's not likely to look for us in here, is he?

ELLIE:
No. Nobody would! Ooh, you have got a cheek, Viv!

VIV:
And aren't you glad!

ELLIE:
Yeah!

ELLIE cranes her neck trying to see what's in the display unit etc.

VIV:

Walk round, have a nosey.

ELLIE:

Do you think she'd mind?

VIV:

You enjoy yourself. Pretend you're at the Ideal Home exhibition.

ELLIE:

It's like that, isn't it? The ideal home.

VIV:

If you enjoy dusting ornaments. Go on, what's the harm?

ELLIE:

I'd better take my shoes off.

Ellie takes off her shoes and then, carrying them with her, she begins to tiptoe round the room, peering at the furniture and objects in the display cabinet - afraid to touch anything.

ELLIE:

They must have loads of money.

VIV:

Oh, yes.

ELLIE:

She seems very nice, though, Gwen. How did you know her name, Viv?

VIV:

I was behind the hedge when . . .

ELLIE:

Oh, you weren't . . you know?

VIV:

No, I wasn't! I heard her husband shouting at her to shut the garage. I'd have clocked him one if he'd shouted at me like that.

ELLIE:

(*not listening*) Isn't that settee gorgeous!

VIV:

I'm not right keen on pink.

ELLIE:

And look at all these crystal glasses!

VIV:

We used to have some a bit like them - Mick's daft auntie gave them to us as a wedding present.

ELLIE:

Oh, yes. What happened to them?

VIV:

What do you think? They got broke.

Ellie looks at VIV and wishes she'd not asked.

ELLIE:

I hope she brings us some biscuits with our cuppa, I'm starving.

VIV:

I wonder how long her husband's away for, he put a case in the boot.

ELLIE:

This carpet's ever so thick, you can wiggle your toes in it.

She goes to take a closer look at an elegant chair.

ELLIE:

Look at this – must be an antique.

Slowly she sits on it but leaps up immediately as she becomes aware of her wet underwear.

ELLIE:

Oh, I'm soaked right through to my pants!

VIV:

Well, come over here and get dry, then, you dafthead.

ELLIE walks over to the fire and warms her front and then her back.

VIV goes to the drinks cabinet and looks inside.

VIV:

Wouldn't mind a drop of rum in my coffee, when it gets here.

ELLIE:

Viv, come out of there!

VIV:

No shortage of anything here!

ELLIE:

No. Her husband must have a good job.

VIV:

We could do all right here.

ELLIE:

What do you mean?

VIV ignores the question and roams around the room, opening drawers, looking in cupboards.

She picks up a fan on display and, playing with it, moves around, adopting seductive and then suggestive poses - making ELLIE laugh.

ELLIE:

I expect they brought that back from their holidays. I wanted to get one when we went to Spain that time, but .

VIV:

(examining the fan) Looks more like an antique than a souvenir to me. They obviously like collecting things - a waste of time to me.

She puts back the fan.

ELLIE:

No, it's nice to have things. I've still got my grandma's toasting fork - the one she said she used to take to bed with her.

VIV:

Didn't do her any good, did it - twelve kids!

ELLIE:

I know! One was enough for me!

VIV:

Yeah. *(Her face hardens before she changes the subject)* Have you warmed up a bit?

ELLIE:

Yeah, it's just my bottom that's still freezing.

VIV:

Well! Nobody's looking!

VIV sits in the armchair by the fire again.

ELLIE hesitates, then pulls up her skirt and sticks her bottom, encased in cheap lacy panties, towards the fire.

VIV grins as ELLIE giggles, wiggling her bottom as she dries herself.

GWEN enters with the drinks and biscuits. ELLIE hastily pushes down her skirt.

GWEN smiles at them both uncertainly, then concentrates on pouring the tea and coffee.

GWEN:

Do you both take sugar?

VIV:

Two, please.

ELLIE:

None for me, thank you. Got to watch my figure.

Tea and coffee served in silence.

GWEN observes them, like two strange creatures, but looks away in embarrassment when they look at her.

VIV is relaxed, ELLIE perches on the edge of the sofa, holding her cup daintily. She gazes longingly at the plate of biscuits. VIV reaches for them.

VIV:

Mind if I have a biscuit?

GWEN:

(reaches to hand them to her) Sorry! Please do help yourselves.

VIV grabs a handful, ELLIE takes one, then another.

ELLIE:

These are good. Marks and Spencer's?

GWEN:

Yes.

ELLIE:

I buy their stuff, sometimes.

VIV:

Oh yeah?

ELLIE:

I do! When I can afford it. *(To GWEN)* Do you buy a lot from M&S?

GWEN:

No. I tend to do my own cooking and baking. Something for me to do.

VIV:

You don't go out to work then?

GWEN:

No.

ELLIE:

I wish I didn't. I've always wanted to stay at home, especially when our Tracy was little.

GWEN:

Oh, you have a daughter?

ELLIE:

Yes.

GWEN:

How old is she?

VIV grins, knowing ELLIE is sensitive about her age.

ELLIE:

Thirty. I was very young when I had her. Have you any children?

GWEN:

A son. James. But he's married now.

VIV:

So there's just you and your husband, is there?

GWEN suspects a motive behind VIV's questions.

GWEN:

Yes.

ELLIE:

He's given you a lovely home.

GWEN:

Well, actually some of the things were mine - well, my parents', I mean.

VIV:

They must have been well off.

GWEN:

Yes. My father worked very hard.

VIV:

Oh, yeah, what did he do?

GWEN doesn't want to answer all these questions, but VIV's unblinking stare demands it.

GWEN:

He built up his own business. Plastic containers.

ELLIE:

(Trying to make a "genteel" joke) But he preferred china really.

I couldn't help noticing your collection.

GWEN:

Oh, the china was my mother's *(indicates the figurine)*- apart from that.

ELLIE:

Oh, did *you* buy that?

GWEN:

No. My husband bought it for me. A kind of joke really.

VIV:

How do you mean?

GWEN:

Well, a sort of model for me to follow. She's called Miss Perfection, you see.

ELLIE:

Oh, that's nice.

VIV:

Is it?

ELLIE:

She does look like you.

GWEN:

Does she?

ELLIE:

Well, in a way, elegant, you know.

VIV drains her cup, puts it down noisily and holds the cup and saucer pointedly on the edge of her lap.

GWEN sees that VIV wants more coffee, but she wants them to leave. She looks at the clock, and gets up.

GWEN:

Well . . .

VIV:

(*holding out her cup and saucer*)   Mind if I have another cup?

GWEN:

No, of course not. *(Pours coffee)*

VIV:

Think it's starting to rain again.

ELLIE:

Oh, it's not, is it?

VIV helps herself to more biscuits, ELLIE follows her example.

GWEN:

Do you have to go out looking for customers, even in this sort of weather?

VIV:

You get used to it. It'd be OK if it were our own business.

GWEN:

Oh, you work for a company.

VIV:

A bloke - I wouldn't call him company, would you, Ellie?

ELLIE:

No! It's like being stuck in a cage with a gorilla, travelling round with him in that van.

VIV:

No, gorillas smell better!

ELLIE:

Yeah! And they've better manners! Oh, if he puts his filthy hands on me again, I'll . . . (*to GWEN*) Oh, I'm sorry.

ELLIE looks down, gripping her cup and saucer.

Silence.

VIV:

We had a bit of an incident on the way here this morning.

GWEN looks at ELLIE, then gently takes her cup and saucer.

GWEN:

Would you like some more tea?

Ellie looks up at her, like a grateful child.

ELLIE:

Please.

ELLIE takes a hankie from her bag and blows her nose. GWEN hands her the tea.

GWEN:

I'll get some more biscuits.

She exits. VIV wanders around the room, and then looks out of the window.

ELLIE:

It's not fair, is it?

VIV:

What?

ELLIE:

Why can't we be like her - with all this? (*she's near to tears*) Oh, Viv I'm fed up! I can't face going back in that van with Jacko.

VIV:

I know. It's a bloody lousy job as well. We're earning nowt!

ELLIE:

Oh, I'd give anything to have a break. A little holiday.

VIV:

(*puts her arm round ELLIE*)   Yeah.

GWEN returns with the biscuits, and is concerned to see that ELLIE is still upset. She picks up the teapot.

GWEN:

Can I . . .?

VIV:

No, we're all right, thanks. Don't want to be looking for a toilet all morning!

They laugh, GWEN hesitantly joining in to be polite.

GWEN:

Yes, I suppose that can be a problem, when you're travelling about. It can't be a very nice job, really, knocking on doors.

VIV:

No, some people get quite stroppy with you. And nobody seems to want their carpets cleaning at the moment. Must be the wrong time of year or summat.

GWEN:

Oh.

ELLIE:

And that's not our fault - but you'd think it was the way Jacko carries on.

VIV:

He'd kill us if he knew we were in here, drinking tea!

ELLIE:

Yeah. Gwen, would you mind if I had a cigarette? I wouldn't normally, but . . .

GWEN:

No, I don't mind - really.

ELLIE gets her cigarettes and lighter out of her bag. The lighter refuses to work.

ELLIE:

Have you got a light?

GWEN looks round for the lighter.

VIV watches her and nods towards the drawer where GWEN hid the lighter.

VIV:

I think it's in there, love.

GWEN, acutely embarrassed, looks at VIV and takes out the lighter. She lights ELLIE's cigarette and then hesitantly puts the lighter back on the table.

VIV:
You don't need to worry, you know, Gwen. We're not going to pinch anything.

GWEN:
Oh, I didn't . . .

She stops the lie as she sees VIV's sardonic smile and decides to make amends for her behaviour by becoming more friendly.

GWEN:
So, where do you come from?

VIV:
Barnsley.

GWEN:
Oh, that's quite a way.

ELLIE enters the game of polite conversation.

ELLIE:
Do you know Barnsley?

GWEN:
No, I'm afraid I haven't been there.

VIV:
You haven't missed much!

ELLIE:
Barnsley's lovely, it's a homely little place.

VIV:
Yeah. Have you lived here long, Gwen?

GWEN:

Yes, about fifteen years. We moved here to be near a good school for James. Oh, that's seems a century ago!

VIV:

Is that 'James' in that photo?

GWEN:

Yes.

VIV gets the photo and shows it to ELLIE.

ELLIE:

Oh, quite good-looking, isn't he?

GWEN:

You should see his wedding photo - he looks even more handsome in that.

ELLIE:

Oh, can I have a look?

GWEN gets the framed photograph from the bureau drawer.

VIV senses progress, and nods encouragement to ELLIE.

GWEN:

(*showing the photo to ELLIE*) He didn't want to wear a top hat and tails really, but Paul insisted. That's Paul, my husband.

VIV:

Ooh, you married a tasty looking fella, didn't you?

ELLIE:

Yeah, I have to be honest, he could even give my Colin a run for his money.

VIV:

Looks quite a charmer. I bet you have to keep an eye on him! You know - other women after him.

GWEN:

No, my husband wouldn't dream of . . .

VIV:

Get on! All men do! They're made that way!

ELLIE:

My Colin isn't!

VIV:

No, but he's not in the same league as this one, is he? Does he go away on business a lot, your husband?

GWEN:

Yes.

VIV:

(*knowingly*) Oh, yeah. Never mind, love.

GWEN:

What do you . . .? Paul is not the kind of man who . . He doesn't . . He . .

VIV:

Oh, sorry, love, we didn't mean to upset you. Forget it - it was the wedding photo we were interested in.

ELLIE:

Yes. And you're right, it is a better one of your James. He's very handsome.

ELLIE admires the photo and holds it to show VIV again. She glances at it with obviously feigned interest.

ELLIE:

It's a fabulous photograph, isn't it, Viv?

VIV:

Yes, very good.

ELLIE:

What a gorgeous dress! And isn't she beautiful, the bride!

GWEN:

Yes, she's a lovely girl.

VIV:

What's she called?

GWEN:

Heather.

ELLIE:

Oh, Heather. Scottish, isn't it, Heather? Tracy's an American name. I got it from 'High Society'. You know, the film, Grace Kelly's part, the rich girl. Colin wasn't so keen, but he gave in in the end.

VIV:

Colin's her husband.

GWEN:

Yes, I realised that.

VIV:

He's a shop-fitter - when he's in work. What does your husband do?

GWEN:

(*to ELLIE*) Do you like the bridesmaids' dresses?

ELLIE:

Oh, yes. Gorgeous colour. Isn't that little one sweet! Did they put the photo in the paper?

GWEN:

Yes.

ELLIE:

They put our Tracy's in. It was a lovely wedding. I was determined it was going to be perfect - and it was, even the weather. Our Tracy had two bridesmaids, her cousin Melanie and . .

VIV:

Yes, all right, Ellie. Don't start giving Gwen every little detail!

GWEN:

Oh, I don't mind.

ELLIE:

See, she's interested.

She turns away from VIV and focuses only on GWEN.

ELLIE:

The other was her best friend, Julie. They wore pale blue with a bit of white lace edging. There was loads of lace on Tracy's dress, and pearls on the tiara - only imitation of course. And we paid for a sit down do in the King's Arms afterwards. Costs a bomb, doesn't it?

GWEN:

Yes, weddings can be rather . . . .

ELLIE:

Worth it, though, to have a dream come true! Have you got an album?

GWEN:

Yes.

ELLIE beams expectantly.

GWEN:

Would you like to see it?

ELLIE:

Ooh, yes please!

GWEN gets the wedding album from a cupboard and sits close to ELLIE.

GWEN:

There are rather a lot of photos, I'm afraid. Just say when you've had enough.

ELLIE:

No, it's lovely. Oh, look at that. Oh, that little page boy is so cute.

VIV sits watching them - and begins to feel a little excluded as ELLIE gives GWEN and the photos all her attention.

ELLIE:

Oh, I love this one - just the two of them under that tree. Look at the way the sunlight catches the satin.

GWEN:

Yes, that's one of my favourites.

ELLIE:

You had a professional photographer, didn't you?

GWEN:

Well, yes.

ELLIE continues to gasp and turn pages.

VIV has seen another older album in the cupboard. She takes it out and begins to leaf through it.

GWEN notices and is not happy about this invasion of privacy, but hasn't the courage to say anything.

ELLIE:
Oh, that's a good one. What were the flowers?
GWEN:
Pink rosebuds and carnations, and . .
ELLIE:
I just had red roses in my bouquet - for love. Did you have any red roses in yours?
GWEN:
No.

VIV looks at her closely.

GWEN feels this scrutiny and glances at VIV, who smiles.

ELLIE:
Oh, Viv come and have a look at all these bridesmaids.

VIV has had enough of weddings. She begins to stack the cups on the tray.

VIV:
I'll get rid of these for you, shall I?

GWEN is alarmed at the idea of VIV wandering round the house.

GWEN:

There's no need. I'll see to them later.

VIV looks at her.

VIV:

I see.

GWEN is again ashamed of her suspicions.

GWEN:

Well, if you don't mind - the kitchen's through there and to the left.

VIV:

(*beams at GWEN*) I know!

She stacks the cups etc. then picks up the tray and exits. ELLIE and GWEN glance up and see her move away. Focusing all their attention on each other now that VIV has gone, and they become more relaxed.

ELLIE:

It was the best day of my life, my wedding day.

GWEN:

Was it?

ELLIE:

Yeah.

Suddenly aware of her less than perfect life, ELLIE hides her emotion by picking up the wedding photo from the coffee table.

ELLIE:

I'll put this back, shall I? Does it go on the bureau?

GWEN:

Yes.

ELLIE gets up and places the photo on the bureau.

ELLIE:

It wasn't a posh wedding like this one. We, had to make do a bit. But it was magic to me.

ELLIE stands very tall and graceful, smoothing an imaginary wedding gown. She and GWEN are focused on each other and don't notice that VIV has quietly come back to stand in the doorway and watch them.

ELLIE:

I felt like a princess in that dress.

GWEN:

I expect you looked like one, too.

ELLIE:

There's a really old song *(half sings)* "This is my lovely day. This is the day I shall remember the day I'm dying"   I used to think that was daft, that last line, but . . .now *(she is suddenly close to tears)* You must think I'm barmy.

GWEN:

No. Come and look at the rest of the album with me.

VIV watches as GWEN makes ELLIE welcome, close beside her on the sofa. VIV, her hands in her cardigan pockets, strolls forward to talk to the audience.

VIV:

Aah, the lady feels sorry for us. (beat) I like that. (*watching ELLIE*) I've tried to tell Ellie what the world's about but she doesn't want to listen.

She reads too many magazines. There's this woman she cleans for who passes the posh ones on to her. 'House and Garden', 'Woman and Home'

Ellie's forever looking for ideas, that little extra touch, something that people will notice.

Some people make a career out of their house, don't they? (*she glances at the window*)

It's still bloody raining. I don't want to go out in that - getting soft in my old age.

I'll go and have another look in the kitchen. Wonder what she was planning to have for her tea - sorry 'dinner'. Or is it 'supper'?

She exits.

ELLIE:

We had a buffet at our wedding, did you?

GWEN:

No, not a buffet.

ELLIE:

We had a dance afterwards as well. And there was a bit of a platform, and a microphone, so my Dad could do a bit of MC-ing. And do you know what I did?

GWEN:

What?

ELLIE:

I sang to my Colin! It must have been the champagne – well a sort of Asti Spumante actually.

She stands, hands clasped in front of her – back in the magic of her wedding day.

I sang 'To know, know, know him' I don't know what the proper title is, do you?

GWEN shakes her head.

ELLIE:

You know the song, though.

GWEN:

I don't think so.

ELLIE:

Oh, you must do! *(sings)* 'To know, know, know him, is to love, love, love him, and I do, and I do, and I do and I do, and I do!' You do remember it, don't you?

GWEN:

Yes, I think so. My parents weren't keen on pop music but I used to have the radio on quietly in my bedroom.

ELLIE:

I saw Brian Poole and the Tremeloes once. They played at this dance at the Locarno ballroom. Did you go to dances at the Locarno?

GWEN:

No, only the ones at school, in the sixth form.

ELLIE:

Ooh, hell, is that all? You haven't lived, have you?

GWEN stares at her. ELLIE is nervous again.

ELLIE:

Sorry! Have I offended you?

GWEN:

No, of course not. I think you may be right, unfortunately.

ELLIE:

That's all right, then. My Mum and Dad weren't keen on me going to the Locarno, really, but where else could you go to meet a fella?

GWEN:

Is that where you met Colin?

ELLIE:

Yeah. Oh, I loved those dances! Hey, I've got a tape in

my bag - Jacko sometimes lets us play tapes in the van. Sixties stuff, shall we put it on?

She gets the tape and heads for the stereo.

GWEN watches bemused as Little Eva's 'The Locomotion' plays, and ELLIE begins to sing, do arm movements and dance.

ELLIE:

Come on, you've got to know this one!

ELLIE gets carried away with the dance. When she sees GWEN smile she holds out her hand to her.

ELLIE:

Come on!

GWEN shakes her head but ELLIE pulls her up and persuades her to join in.

ELLIE:

It's dead easy. Just follow me.

GWEN is at first reluctant and embarrassed but then begins to enjoy it.

VIV enters and GWEN stops dancing when she sees her, but VIV pushes her steadily back into line.

VIV:

Go on, humour her. Make her happy - it costs nowt!

GWEN finds VIV's smile and physical force hard to resist, and dances again, but is not as relaxed now.

ELLIE continues to dance, showing off a little.

The music changes to Manfred Mann "Do wah diddy diddy" as VIV moves forward to talk to the audience in a friendly, confiding manner.

ELLIE dances towards the audience and the light fades out on the set behind her.

VIV:

She always was a good dancer, little Ellie - and she knew it. A lot of lads fancied her, she was a pretty little kid - still is.

A mirror ball is switched on as ELLIE dances closer to the audience and is gradually caught up in lights of a dance hall.

VIV:

That dance hall was her fantasy land, where she could grab a few moments of feeling special.

VIV takes on the role of the compere/disc jockey at the dance and mimes speaking into a microphone.

COMPERE/VIV:

That's right girls, walk down that street, show 'em what you're made of!
(*sings*) 'She looked good! She looked fine!'
Come on, lads! You've had enough Dutch courage by now surely. Get on the floor and give these lovely girls a thrill!

The music and lights continue. The music changes to Roy Orbison's 'Pretty Woman'.

Do your best dancing now, girls, because this is the time for us to choose our Dancing Queen of the night. Turn on that spotlight, Pete, and let's search for our lucky little lady.

A spotlight circles and ELLIE dances flamboyantly, trying to keep in the light, obviously craving to be chosen.

The COMPERE/VIV advances towards her with a microphone.

COMPERE/VIV:

Could it be this young lady here? What's your name, sweetheart?

ELLIE:

(*young and breathless*) Ellie. Eleanor.

COMPERE/VIV:

You're a great little dancer.

ELLIE:

Oh.

COMPERE/VIV:

Have you got a steady boyfriend, Ellie?

ELLIE:

Yes.

COMPERE/VIV:

And what's his name?

ELLIE:

Colin.

COMPERE/VIV:

And has Colin popped the question yet?

ELLIE:

(Giggles) No.

COMPERE/VIV:

Does he like chocolates?

ELLIE:

Yes.

COMPERE/VIV:

Well, he's going to love you tonight then because I'm going to present you with this great big box of Cadbury's Milk Tray.

ELLIE:

Oh!

COMPERE/VIV:

Yes, Ellie, you are - our Dancing Queen of the night!

ELLIE mimes taking the box of chocolates.

ELLIE:

Oh, thanks!   Thank you!   Thank you!

COMPERE/VIV:

Take a bow, Ellie!

ELLIE curtsies, dances and curtsies again, gradually moving back out of the spotlight which fades out.

VIV:

She lived for moments like that, did Ellie. Still does, but there haven't been any for a long time.

Full lighting on the set again, and ELLIE is back dancing in front of GWEN, who now sits on the sofa watching her.

VIV:

That box of chocolates didn't last long, not with four brothers and sisters. They weren't a bad family, but they'd no bloody money.

VIV watches ELLIE showing off to GWEN

VIV:

She likes to give the impression she had a posh wedding, does Ellie. Well, it were a second hand dress and the 'reception' was sandwiches and sausage rolls in the Sunday school hall.

She was convinced Colin was 'Mr Right' - still is - but he'd no money either. Ellie could have done a lot better than him. I told her that, but she wouldn't listen to me.

The tape stops.

ELLIE:

Oh, yeah, that's the last track on that side. Shall I turn it over?

VIV:

In a bit, love. Did you like going dancing, Gwen?

ELLIE:

Her parents wouldn't let her.

VIV:

(*sitting on the sofa beside GWEN*)   Oh, what a shame. Me and Ellie used to go every Saturday night. Ellie always had loads of lads after her!

ELLIE:

Yeah, it was great. I met Colin at a Valentine's Dance. Where did you meet Paul?

GWEN:

At a party. My parents introduced him to me.

ELLIE:

And it was love at first sight, I bet!

GWEN looks away.

ELLIE:

How long was it before you got married?

GWEN:

Two years.

ELLIE:

Two years! Oh, you were keen weren't you!

Seeing GWEN's reaction ELLIE corrects herself.

ELLIE:

I mean, you must have known each other really well by the time you got married.

GWEN:

I suppose so.

VIV:

But you never really know them till you get into bed with them, do you?

GWEN's embarrassment is observed by ELLIE.

ELLIE:

Viv! Shurrup!

VIV is surprised and a little annoyed at being told off by ELLIE, but ELLIE makes amends with a wink and a smile.

Then VIV is again perturbed as she watches ELLIE perch on the arm of the sofa and put her arm round GWEN.

ELLIE:

You're romantic like me, aren't you, Gwen?

GWEN smiles at her. VIV again is aware of feeling excluded and decides to assert herself. She walks over to finger the decanter on the drinks cabinet.

VIV:

Nice drop of whisky is it?

GWEN refuses to take the hint.

ELLIE feels a little uncomfortable at VIV's pushiness.

ELLIE:

Oh, you know, I used to dream about who I'd meet at those Saturday night dances.

GWEN:

Did you?

VIV:

Oh, yes. And from the Saturday night she'd dream about the lad she'd met - until about Wednesday. Then she'd start to dream about the one she was going to meet next Saturday!

ELLIE:

Well, you want to have a good look at what's on offer before you make your mind up.

VIV:

(*a bad memory*) Or have it made up for you.

GWEN looks at her.

VIV:

Shall I make us something to eat?

GWEN:

(*Lying*) Well, actually I have to go out, soon.

VIV:

Oh?

GWEN:

Yes.

ELLIE:

Oh, we'd better be going then. We don't want to be any trouble.

GWEN:

Oh, you're not!

VIV:

Oh, well, if you're sure, we'll stop until we get dried off properly. Ellie's worse than me.

ELLIE:

No, I'm all right.

VIV:

Rubbish. (*to GWEN*) You can see she's soaked to the skin, can't you?

GWEN:

Oh.

ELLIE:

No, I'm O K.

VIV's stare demands that ELLIE should follow her lead.

VIV:

No, you're not. You're certainly in no fit state to get back in that van, are you?

ELLIE:

(*trying to read VIV*)   No.

VIV:

Gwen, could you lend her something to put on, so we can get her clothes dry?

GWEN:

Yes. Yes, I suppose so. I'll . .

She goes towards the stairs.

VIV:

We'll come upstairs with you, shall we?

GWEN:

No, no there's no need, I'll bring some clothes down.

VIV:

But she'll need to try them on, you don't know her size - she's very deceptive - size-wise I mean.

GWEN:

No, I think I can find something.

VIV:

We don't both need to come up, if you don't want. Just Ellie, eh?

GWEN hesitates

VIV:

It'd be a real treat for her.

ELLIE:

Yeah. I love looking at clothes. Do you like clothes?

GWEN:

Yes. I suppose I do.

ELLIE:

Oh, I bet you've got some lovely things.

VIV lays her arm heavily but mock- affectionately round GWEN's shoulder

VIV:

Go on, love, show her.

GWEN is startled by VIV's closeness but doesn't move away.

GWEN:

All right.

ELLIE is delighted as she follows GWEN upstairs

VIV watches them and then goes to help herself to a whisky from the cabinet. She turns again to the audience.

VIV:

Nice, isn't she, Gwen? Too nice for her own good. She probably thinks that if you're nice to people it'll make them like you.
It hasn't worked with her husband, though. He didn't even look at her when he set off - he'd have made more fuss of the dog, if they had one.
That's what you need these days, isn't it, a big guard dog to look after you - or a big fella. We wouldn't have lasted two minutes here if her husband had been in.

Didn't want me wandering round her house, did she? Pity, I'd have liked a look - clothes tell you a lot about people.
Hey, how about a fashion show - let's put Gwendolyn Courtney on the catwalk, eh? Gwendolyn, what a bloody name!

The lights change. Count Basie's 'Lady Be Good' is played in the background as GWEN appears in a spotlight as if walking down a catwalk

VIV gives a commentary – in the husky tones of a fashion show compere.

COMPERE/VIV:
And here we have day wear for the middle aged, middle class housewife on her 'at home' days. Gwen is suitably attired in a soft navy skirt, worn well below the knee. Her husband doesn't like her to wear anything too revealing.

GWEN does a twirl, and then pulls her cardigan closer

This used to confuse Gwen a little, when she saw him admiring other women's legs and cleavages. However, she now comforts herself with the embrace of her lambs' wool cardigan - in a toning shade of Tory blue.
Harmony is everything.

GWEN stands still and isolated in the spotlight.

The top is carefully styled to avoid any embarrassing suggestion of motherhood or, dare we mention it, sexuality.

GWEN exits.

VIV watches her leave and then, back in character, picks up the family photo album again. She opens it and turns to the audience.

VIV:
You wouldn't have caught Gwen's mother in an outfit like that (*turns a page*) Liked to show she had a bit of, brass, did that old bag - you can see that from the photos.
You can see she kept Gwen well in line as well, preferably on the back row when it came to photos.
Some people don't like competition, do they? The problem for daughters like Gwen is that they never quite kick the habit of doing what Mummy and Daddy tell them. Like marrying Paul Courtney. Money came into that as well, I expect.

She puts down the album as ELLIE skips in and does a twirl to show off what she's wearing - a black velvet skirt, a pink 'designer' sweater and a gold pendant.

ELLIE:

Look what she's lent me? Aren't they fabulous! You should see what she's got up there. Two wardrobes full of clothes and it's nearly all designer labels and Marks and Spencer's!

VIV:

Where is she?

ELLIE:

Gone to the loo. I went as well while I was up there. The bathroom's gorgeous, white and peachy pink. There's no gold taps though - but the towels are so soft and fluffy it seemed a shame to wet them.

VIV:

You like it here, don't you, love?

ELLIE:

Ooh, yeah! Oh, you don't realise do you that people really live like this?

VIV:

It's in all them magazines you read.

ELLIE:

Yes, I know but it's real this. I mean she lives here, every day.

VIV:

With her rich husband.

ELLIE:

Oh, he's hardly ever here! Like he's away on this business trip now.

VIV:

How long for?

ELLIE:

Quite a while I think - he's gone to Paris and then it's New York!

VIV:

She must get lonely, here on her own.

ELLIE:

Yes. But I wouldn't mind being lonely in a place like this!

VIV:

I think she could do with a bit of company.

ELLIE:

Yes, I suppose she could.

VIV:

So we'll stop on for a bit, shall we?

ELLIE:

Stay here? She won't want us staying here!

VIV:

She will.

ELLIE:

How can we? I mean, Jacko will be looking for us.

VIV:

Like I said, he won't come here - but we mustn't let her know that.

ELLIE:

Why not?

GWEN enters - more relaxed.

VIV:

(to Ellie) Just follow me.

VIV:

Doesn't she look nice! It's ever so kind of you, Gwen.

GWEN:

It's a pleasure.

VIV:

Yes. It's nice, isn't it, this? All girls together, eh? Nothing like a bit of company, is there? Other women to talk to.

She nods to ELLIE who eventually takes the hint

ELLIE:

Oh, yes. I don't know what I'd do sometimes without Viv and my mates. When things get you down, you need to talk, don't you?

GWEN:

Yes.

VIV:

Who do you talk to?

GWEN has no answer

ELLIE:

I bet you've got loads of friends round here.

GWEN:

Oh, yes.

ELLIE:

Who's your best friend? You know, the one you tell your secrets to?

GWEN:

You don't tell secrets.

ELLIE:

Oh, no. .

VIV:

We need to tell you something − a sort of secret.

GWEN:

Oh.

VIV:

We didn't want to say anything, but the truth is we need your help.

ELLIE takes her cue from VIV and nods at GWEN.

VIV:

You see, we're frightened. This Jacko, he's giving us a lot of grief. He won't leave Ellie alone, even when I'm with her. And like we told you, he's a big bloke.

GWEN:

Oh.

VIV:

We're desperate to get away from him. That's why we ran to your house. So what we're asking is, can we hide here for a bit? It won't be for long.

ELLIE:

Please, can we stay, just for an hour or two?

GWEN:

Well, yes I suppose so, but . . .

VIV gives her a hug. GWEN, unused to such warmth, finds herself smiling at her.

VIV:

Ooh, you are a love! I tell you what - I'll make us some of my special sandwiches.

ELLIE:

Oh, yes, can she? She makes great sandwiches - she puts all sorts in them.

GWEN:

Well . . .

VIV:

Won't take me two minutes!

Exits to the kitchen

ELLIE:

She's great is Viv.

GWEN:

Have you been friends for a long time?

ELLIE:

On and off. We lost touch a bit after we got married - my Colin didn't like Mick, Viv's husband. Ex- husband.

GWEN:

Oh, they got divorced?

ELLIE:

Yeah, but not quick enough! She still has a scar where he threw that iron at her.

GWEN:

He threw an iron at her?

ELLIE:

Yeah, red hot it was. She threw it straight back of course. But it must be terrible to have a violent husband.

GWEN:

Yes.

ELLIE:

My Colin's the gentlest man you could ever meet. You count yourself lucky when you've married a good man, don't you?

GWEN smiles – unconvincingly.

ELLIE:

I mean you feel you've achieved something, don't you - a happy marriage, children. All a woman ever wants, isn't it?

GWEN is uncomfortable with the subject

GWEN:

Would you like a sherry or a gin and tonic, or something?

ELLIE:

Oh, a gin and tonic please.

GWEN pours the drink - ELLIE watches

ELLIE:

Have you any cherries? I love having a cherry to swizzle.

GWEN finds the cocktail cherries and hands her the drink

ELLIE:

Aren't you having one?

GWEN:

Oh, no, I don't . . . Yes. Yes, I think I will.

GWEN pours herself a little gin with plenty of tonic

ELLIE relaxes into the good life on the sofa

ELLIE:

I feel sorry for Viv, sometimes. She never had any kids, you know. And she loves mothering people.

GWEN:

Does she?

ELLIE:

Oh, yes, real protective. (*remembering their story*) Like this business with Jacko - I'd have had it if she hadn't looked after me.

ELLIE goes to the window, watching for Jacko.

GWEN:

Do you think he'll still be looking for you?

ELLIE:

Ooh, yes! He'll be round our house tonight, frightening the neighbours. I'll have to stay away till he gets fed up of looking.

GWEN:

Won't your husband deal with him?

ELLIE:

He's away at the moment. Like yours. When will your husband be back?

GWEN:

I'm not sure.

ELLIE:

It's not fair, is it, him leaving you on your own. Don't you get lonely? I would.

GWEN:

Yes. I suppose I do.

ELLIE:

(*gives GWEN a hug*) Well, you're not lonely today, are you! You've got us here! Oh, I feel really wicked, drinking during the day. And gin and tonic – I usually have a Cinzano.

GWEN:

Oh, I don't think we have that, but we do have Martini if you'd prefer it?

ELLIE:

No, this is lovely – it's what they drink on tele, isn't it? They always talk about having a G & T. Shall we have another?

GWEN:

Yes, why not!

GWEN is pouring drinks with ELLIE fussing round her as VIV enters with a tray of hefty sandwiches - thickly sliced bread stuffed with cheese, salad etc.

VIV immediately walks forward to talk to the audience

VIV:

Nothing but bloody salad stuff in that fridge! She's got some lamb chops in the freezer, though. They'll do for tonight. Oh, yes, don't worry we'll still be here. How's she going to get rid of us, eh?
The police wouldn't want to know - after all she invited us in, and we're not doing any harm, are we?
And anyway, I don't think she'll want us to go really. What woman wants to be alone in a house at night these days?

Nobody wants to be on their own. But we all are, aren't we - really. I learned that a long time ago.

She fixes on a bright smile and walks towards ELLIE and GWEN, presenting the tray with a flourish.

ELLIE:

Oh, great, I'm starving.

ELLIE gets up and makes a grab towards the sandwiches.

VIV pulls the tray away from her.

VIV:

Manners!

ELLIE sits down, embarrassed. VIV gives her a plate and then offers a plate and the sandwiches to GWEN.

VIV:

You'll have to excuse us. We haven't had the advantage of a decent upbringing like you.

GWEN:

(*passing the sandwiches to ELLIE*) Please do help yourself.

VIV:

Aren't you having one? I washed my hands you know!

GWEN reluctantly takes a sandwich. ELLIE also takes one and eats hungrily.

VIV stands apart, a sandwich in her hand, but watching them.

VIV:

When you come from a big family you learn to grab things quick or you miss out. Have you any brothers or sisters?

GWEN:

No. My father would have liked a son, but I don't think my mother wanted any more children.

ELLIE:

(*laughs with her mouth full*) Once is enough for some things, isn't it! I had a really hard time having our Tracy - never again, I said, and I meant it! Ooh, it was . . . .

VIV:

All right, Ellie - we don't want the gory details. Did you just have James?

GWEN:

Yes.

VIV:

I bet his grandparents spoil him to death.

GWEN:

Yes, they did.

VIV:

Oh. Passed on, have they?

GWEN nods.

VIV:

So there's just you and your husband now. No relatives?

GWEN:

Only Paul's sister.

VIV:
And where does she live?

GWEN is not happy about all these questions.

ELLIE sees this and is embarrassed.

ELLIE:
Don't be nosey, Viv.

VIV glares at her.

VIV:
Just making conversation. I like talking to people, don't you, Gwen?

GWEN:
Yes.

VIV strolls round the room. She pauses by the bureau and moves the figure of the Edwardian lady dangerously close to the edge.

Gwen watches this a little anxiously.

ELLIE is aware of her anxiety.

ELLIE:
Capo di Monte, isn't it, that?

GWEN:
No. Royal Doulton.

VIV smiles at GWEN, and takes hold of the figurine.

GWEN is not happy at the way she handles it.

VIV notices and enjoys making GWEN nervous.

VIV:

You know this is marvellous for us, to be able to sit in a lovely room like this with someone like you to talk to. Usually we only see rooms like this on the tele, don't we, Ellie?

ELLIE:

Yeah. It's fabulous.

VIV:

I wonder if you realise how lucky you are?

GWEN:

Oh, I think I do.

VIV places the figurine on the edge of the bureau.

VIV:

It's very kind of you to share it with us for a little while. Of course, if we're any trouble you only have to say so and we'll go.

GWEN:

No, you're very welcome.

VIV pushes the figurine slowly back into a slightly safer position and moves away towards the window.

GWEN:

But I do have to go out this afternoon.

VIV stiffens and stares hard at GWEN.

VIV:

Anywhere special?

GWEN pauses, searching for a lie.

VIV observes this, and smiles at her.

VIV:

Nice to have a trip out. Got your own little car have you?

GWEN:

Yes.

ELLIE:

Oh, you are lucky. I can't even drive.

VIV:

Well, lessons cost money, don't they? We like going out, don't we, Ellie?

ELLIE:

Yeah.

VIV:

You won't be staying out late, though, will you, Gwen?

It's not nice coming back to an empty house in the dark, or even in the daylight if it comes to that. Have you ever been burgled?

GWEN:

Yes. A few months ago.

VIV:

What did they pinch?

GWEN:

Some of my jewellery, and one of Paul's computers.

ELLIE:

Oh, how awful. You weren't in, were you?

GWEN:

No.

VIV:

You were lucky, then. Not like that poor woman in the paper the other week.

ELLIE:

Oh, yes, that was horrible.

GWEN:

We've had a new alarm system fitted now . . .

VIV:

So did that woman - and a phone in the bedroom - but it didn't stop them.

ELLIE:

Did the police catch the ones who broke into your house?

GWEN:

No.

VIV:

Typical.

ELLIE:
And did the burglars come back? They do sometimes, to get the rest of your stuff.

GWEN:
Yes. They've been back, I'm pretty sure they have. I hear noises in the night. They always come when Paul's away. I've phoned the police but they . . . .

VIV:
Don't want to know, do they?

GWEN:
No.

ELLIE:
I expect they think you're making it up.

GWEN:
That's the impression I get.

VIV:
Well, just you be careful when you come home tonight. We'll be off as soon as we've had these sandwiches.

ELLIE is disappointed, GWEN relieved.

VIV:
I'll make a pot of tea to go with them −if you don't mind.

GWEN:
Oh.

VIV:

Won't be long. (*exits*)

GWEN gets up and, trying to make the action look casual, moves the china figure back to its original position.

She stands looking at the photo of her son.

ELLIE:

It must be great having your own car, being able to go off where you want. I wish me and Colin could.

GWEN:

Does your husband not drive?

ELLIE:

Oh, yes, he drives the firm's van. We borrow it sometimes. Our car's off the road at the moment. Colin's going to fix it soon. He knows I can't stand not being able to go out. I expect you go out a lot.

GWEN:

Not really. I get wheeled out for appearances from time to time.

ELLIE:

You what?

GWEN:

Business dinners, that sort of thing.

ELLIE:

Oh. I bet that's good.

GWEN shrugs, then looks thoughtfully at ELLIE.

GWEN:

I was brought up to be 'a good listener', were you?

ELLIE:

I don't know, but I'm a good talker - I could talk for England, Colin says. I'm interested in people, if that's what you mean. I buy 'Hello' every week. Colin says it's a waste of money.

GWEN:

The people I meet aren't interested in other people - just themselves.

ELLIE:

Oh, that's not nice.

GWEN:

I suddenly realised I spent whole evenings talking to our so-called friends, and not once had they asked anything about me or my life. And not even about James. Since I realised that, I don't enjoy going out any more.

ELLIE:
I'd like to know about James. Where does he live?

GWEN:
(*sits down near ELLIE*) In a village near Cambridge. They've bought lovely old house, but it needs a lot of renovation.

ELLIE:
That'll cost a bit.

GWEN:
Yes. They're having to do some of the work themselves until James can earn more money.

ELLIE:
What does he do?

GWEN:
Not a lot, according to his father. Paul wanted him to be a barrister, you see.

ELLIE:
A barrister!

GWEN:
James did take a law degree, but it wasn't what he really wanted to do. And he'd met Heather at university, and .

ELLIE:
They wanted to get married.

GWEN:

Yes, straight after university. So James decided to take this job in an estate agents.

ELLIE:

Oh, that sounds good.

GWEN:

His father doesn't think so. He's hardly spoken to him since. Not that they talked much before that.

ELLIE:

Oh, there's a lot of that about, isn't there - fathers and sons.

VIV runs into the room, panic stricken.

VIV:

Get down! Hide! Quick! Jacko's here!

ELLIE squeals with fright and dives flat on the floor hiding below the sofa, dragging GWEN with her.

VIV stands at the side of the window, her back flattened against the wall, as if she's terrified.

She looks at GWEN and ELLIE cowering with their backs to her.

VIV smiles slowly and makes a thumbs up sign to the audience.

END OF ACT ONE.

ACT TWO

SCENE ONE

VIV stretches out on the sofa, a glass of whisky on a table beside her. She's wearing the same skirt ,sweater and cardigan.

VIV.
Yes, we're still here. Well she couldn't chuck us out on the street with Jacko waiting for us, could she? Then it go a bit late, we'd missed the last bus, and . .well, she likes Ellie. Everybody does.

She gets up, takes her glass to the drinks cabinet and pours herself another whisky.

The Lady Gwendolyn's soft, that's her problem. And scared. She's never come into real contact with the likes of us before. Mummy and Daddy were very careful with her like that. Money sticks with money - you know. *(She looks round the room)*
It makes you sick, her and her husband having all this while some of can't afford to keep warm, never mind owt else.

She opens a drawer and idly rummages through the contents while sipping her whisky.

Still, mustn't complain, eh? Keep your problems to yourself or some television lot'll come along and make a bloody documentary about you.

VIV wanders over to the window

VIV.
Look at the size of that garden. She's got her own bloody private park - I wonder where the flaming swings are?
(*smiles confidingly*) I reckon we can 'swing it' for a couple more nights here if we work it right. I really had Ellie going yesterday, poor kid. She spent half the night peeping out from behind the curtains, terrified Jacko was going to break in.
Mind you, you can't blame her - he'd made his mind up he was going to get his leg over, even if he had to knock me out first.
He's a nasty piece of work is Jacko, that's why she hasn't said anything to Colin - Jacko'd cripple him if he said owt, and, well, there was the money.
It's gone beyond that now, though, we'll have to start looking again - though God knows where.

But what the hell, forget it. Ellie thinks she's in heaven staying here. Let's hope I can make it last a bit.

VIV wanders round the room, obviously bored. She hears a door close, and footsteps. Quickly she puts the whisky glass back in the cabinet.

GWEN enters, smiling.

GWEN:
Ellie wants a cup of tea. Would you like one?

VIV:
No thanks. Is she still in the bath?

GWEN:
No. I'm doing her hair for her.

VIV:
That's very kind of you.

GWEN:
I'm enjoying it.

VIV:
It's just what she needs at the moment, to be made a fuss of. Things have been pretty bad for Ellie lately.

GWEN:
Oh, I'm sorry.

VIV:
She won't have told you.

GWEN:

No.

VIV:

Family problems. I don't know quite what's at the bottom of it, but like she said, her husband's gone away.

GWEN:

Yes, on a fishing holiday, staying with his brother.

VIV:

That's what she's telling everybody, but I think there's a bit more to it than that.

GWEN:

Oh, dear.

VIV:

Anyway, she's thrilled to bits to be staying here. It's really cheered her up. I'm very grateful to you.

GWEN:

Oh. It's no trouble. Ellie's so sweet.

VIV decides this is the moment.

VIV:

Yeah. Actually, she - she's too shy to ask herself - but Ellie's desperate to stay another night. Would that be 'terribly inconvenient'?

GWEN:

Well, . .

VIV:

Oh, that's wonderful! *(Hugs her)* You're a saint! Just one more night, that's all she needs. You've made such a difference to her already!

GWEN:

Well, actually, my husband . . .

VIV:

He won't mind. He'll be glad you've got some company instead of being here on your own. Oh, it's restored my faith in human nature, meeting you.

GWEN stands hesitating as she tries to take in what's happened, and wondering how she can extricate herself from this situation.

VIV:

Ellie'll be wondering where you've got to with that tea.

GWEN:

Oh, yes. I'll make it now.

VIV:

I'll change my mind. I will have a drink - coffee. Two sugars - and shall we have some chocolate biscuits?

Gwen, still dazed, nods and hurries out. VIV grins triumphantly..

Yes!! Easy when you know how, isn't it? Ellie'll be gob-smacked I've fixed it for us to stay on. She nearly fainted last night when I told her Jacko hadn't been near the place. I had to tell her or she wouldn't have slept a wink, poor kid.

(She picks up the Edwardian lady.) Who's the lady of the house now, then? Did you see the way she toddled off to make my coffee? *(clicks her fingers)* Two sugars, and chocolate biscuits. And that's not all I'll have off you, lady.

(She puts the figurine back and puts one finger up at it)
Silly cow! Bet she still goes to church on Sundays - what bloody good does that do! Charity begins at home, they say, well, it will here.

She sprawls on the sofa again, and looks round restlessly.

I'm only giving it one more night, though, else I'll be bored out of my head.
(She sits up, stretches her arms along the back of the sofa and looks around proudly in a proprietorial manner) She'll never forget this, though, won't Ellie.

The lights fade.

SCENE TWO

The lounge is now more "lived in" - slightly untidy, with magazines on the chairs and floor, a sweater over one end of the sofa, a pile of photograph albums, coffee cups.

ELLIE, wearing a white and gold leisure outfit slightly too big for her, dances to a tape. The music is Johnny Burnette's 'You're Sixteen' ELLIE's in a world of her own and happier than she's been for a long time.

The next track is 'The Great Pretender' The Platters - ELLIE starts to dance to it slowly and sexily, starts to sing the lyrics but halts when she comes to "Oh, yes, I'm the great pretender" – she giggles guiltily. She fast-forwards the tape.

VIV enters, bored and irritable. She has an unopened letter in her hand. She winces as the music starts again.

ELLIE switches it off.

ELLIE:
Sorry. Have you still got your headache?
VIV:
I'm all right.
ELLIE:
Why don't you ask Gwen for an aspirin?
VIV:
Ellie, if I want a bloody aspirin I'll just help myself.

VIV holds the letter up to the light.

ELLIE:

What's that?

VIV:

The post's just been. A letter from Cambridge. Addressed just to her, not to him.

ELLIE:

Oh, it must be from James. I'll take it to her, shall I?

VIV:

(props the letter in front of the figurine) No, why should you? You're not her servant, you know. We're her guests, she should be running round after us.

ELLIE wants to take the letter but doesn't want to annoy VIV

VIV:

What's she up to anyway? She were tripping around in the kitchen and lah laahing to Radio 2.

ELLIE:

She's doing us a special meal. A dinner party - four courses and wine.

VIV:

Steak and chips'll do me.

ELLIE:

Oh, we're having steak - steak Diane - for the main course, and I asked if we could have prawn cocktail for the starter, I love prawns. It's a special treat - before we go home.

VIV:

Oh, I see, the Last Supper, eh?

ELLIE:

No. Like I said, it's a dinner party. We're going to dress up.

VIV:

Oh, are we?

VIV sprawls on the sofa again, watching ELLIE.

VIV:

Have you phoned your Colin yet?

ELLIE:

No.

VIV:

Why not? You said he was due back this morning - from his 'fishing holiday'. He'll be worried about you. Phone him now.

ELLIE looks away, picks up a magazine.

VIV:

What's going on? Usually you're wittering if you're away from him for five minutes. Why won't you phone him?

ELLIE:

He'll be at work.

VIV:

No, you said he had the rest of the week off. *(Sits up and glares at ELLIE)* Don't lie to me, Ellie. Every other bugger lies to me - don't you start! Has he left you?

ELLIE:

No! Colin wouldn't leave me. And I wouldn't leave him - he's my husband.

VIV:

Mick was my husband but I left him - thank god!

She thumps a cushion and tries to settle down again.

ELLIE:

There's a big difference between me and Colin and you and Mick!

VIV:

Oh, yeah?

ELLIE:

It's special, me and Colin. Always has been.

VIV:

Oh, special are you?

(*she sits up again and leans forward to look ELLIE up and down*)

Oh, of course you are – I can see that, now you've had your hair done and her ladyship's dolled you up in some of her fancy clothes.

ELLIE:

Well! I wanted to look nice.

VIV:

What for? There's nobody to see you here? (PAUSES) Except her. But, that's it, isn't it? You want to make an impression on the Lady Gwendolyn, don't you?

ELLIE:

No.

VIV:

Yes, you do! You've done nothing but dance round her ever since we got here. She's nothing 'special', you know – just because she's got money. She's no different from you and me – you know, two arms, two legs, two boobs!

ELLIE:

Don't be crude.

VIV:

Oh, I'm crude now, am I? Any other little faults you'd like to mention - or am I not worth the bother of telling?

ELLIE:

Oh, what are you going on like this for? Just because me and Gwen get on.

VIV:

Oh, you get on, do you? You'll be telling me she's your friend next!

ELLIE:

She could be. Me and Gwen could be good friends actually. We have a lot in common. She likes nice things, like I do. And there's her James and my Tracy.

VIV:

Ooh, yes! And her husband and your husband - perhaps you could make up a foursome!

ELLIE:

Don't be daft! Anyway I don't like the sound of her Paul. I don't think she's happy with him. I mean, he hasn't even phoned her to let her know he got there all right.

VIV helps herself to a whisky

VIV:

What does he do, do you know?

ELLIE:

He's a tax consultant.

VIV:

Oh. Great! Helping the rich dodge out of paying tax. A wonderful contribution to the economic welfare of the country!

ELLIE:

Oh, I don't know about all that. But I don't think you should be knocking back his whisky like you are doing.

VIV:

(gets up) Oh, I've had enough of this, we're going!

ELLIE:

Oh, no, Viv - not yet. One more night, you promised!

VIV:

You don't have to come with me. You stop here.

ELLIE:

No, not on my own.

She scampers over to VIV and hangs on to her arm

ELLIE:

Please let's stay, Viv, it's a dream come true is this for me. I've looked at houses like this in magazines for years, and now I'm living in one. It's, an experience, Viv. Something to tell people about. Don't spoil it, Viv, please.

VIV:

You're like a little kid, you. All right - we'll stop - but we're off tomorrow!

ELLIE throws her arms round VIV, who, not used to being hugged, savours the embrace for a moment.

ELLIE:

Oh, I love you!

VIV, embarrassed, pushes her away

VIV:

Gerroff, you daft thing!

ELLIE:

Ooh, isn't it great being here! I think I'll just tidy up a bit. We want it looking nice for this evening, don't we?

VIV yawns and stretches, and sips her whisky, revelling in the luxury.

ELLIE:

Do you mind if I have my tape on again? Only quiet.

VIV:

If you want.

ELLIE plays the Everly Brothers 'That's Old Fashioned' and flits around, taking pleasure in tidying the room.

VIV watches her, then she props herself up on one elbow and turns to the audience.

VIV:
```
Just look at her - she thinks she's in
Fairyland.
Ellie Marshall, the everyday housewife.
She's a throwback to those 1950s 'Good
Housewife' books is Ellie.  She used to buy
all sorts for the house.  She's had to stop
buying stuff now, though.
```

VIV stands and walks towards the audience, the lights behind her and the music fading gradually during this speech.

VIV:
```
But the trouble with Ellie is, she hasn't
learned to stop wanting things.  She's the
sort they get on those game shows.  (pauses)
Let's have a laugh, shall we?
```

A jazzy fanfare and lights flashing as VIV takes on the role of a game show compere.

COMPERE/VIV:
```
And our next contestant on 'Lifestyle
Challenge' is Mrs Colin Marshall!
```

ELLIE teeters hesitantly into the spotlight and the scene continues at a breakneck pace against a background of razzamatazz and applause.

COMPERE/VIV:
Well, good evening, Mrs Marshall! And how are you?

ELLIE bemused and blinking in the spotlight smiles at the compere and at the audience,

ELLIE:
Very well, thank you.

COMPERE/VIV:
Well, I must say you're looking gorgeous in that outfit? Bought it specially for the show, did you?

ELLIE:
No, it's not mine, I borrowed . . . .

COMPERE/VIV:
Is this your first time on television?

ELLIE:
Yes.

COMPERE/VIV:
Well, as we all know (*nudges her*) there's a first time for everything.

ELLIE laughs politely and nervously.

COMPERE/VIV:

Now, have I got the name right - Eleanor Marshall?

ELLIE:

Yes.

COMPERE/VIV:

A very classy name, Eleanor.

ELLIE:

My Mum named me after Eleanor Powell - you know the tap dancer, with Fred Astaire - my Mum loved the old Hollywood films. *(notices the compere's lack of interest)* But everyone calls me Ellie.

COMPERE/VIV:

Right. Ellie. And you're a sales assistant in a department store.

ELLIE:

Well, I was, but they had to do a re-structuring and . .

COMPERE/VIV:

Oh. Well, on with the show, as they say! Now, don't be nervous, Ellie, all you have to do is answer these simple questions that I'm going to put to you. All right?

ELLIE nods again nervously. The razzamatazz increases as COMPERE/VIV delivers the questions at a fast pace.

COMPERE/VIV:

Did you work hard at school, Ellie?

ELLIE:

Yes.

COMPERE/VIV:

The right answer! Did you marry for love or for money?

ELLIE:

Love.

COMPERE/VIV:

Right answer! Did you manage to save up the deposit for a house?

ELLIE:

Eventually.

COMPERE/VIV:

Good answer! Have you worked hard all your life?

ELLIE:

When I could get a job, yes.

COMPERE/VIV:

The right answer! Do you now own your own home?

ELLIE:

No. We've had to sell it.

COMPERE/VIV:

That's correct. Have you been on holiday in the last three years?

ELLIE:

Not a proper holiday, no.

COMPERE/VIV:

Now, Ellie, one more question.

There is a hushed silence.

COMPERE/VIV:

And you must get this answer right if you want to win.
Ellie, what do you want more than anything else in the world?

ELLIE:

My own home, a happy marriage, a nice little job - to be happy, that's all.

COMPERE/VIV:

(PAUSE) Oh, I'm so sorry, Ellie. That's too much to ask for. It's the wrong answer!

ELLIE, almost in tears backs out of the spotlight.

The COMPERE/VIV applauds as the lights return to normal

COMPERE/VIV:

Give her a big round of applause, ladies and gentlemen! Never mind, Ellie, we can't all be lucky!

A pause. VIV, back in character, turns to the audience.

VIV:
Can we?

She stares hard at the audience for a few seconds, then the Everly Brothers are heard again. The lights fade up again as ELLIE puts cups on a tray and plumps up cushions.

GWEN enters.

GWEN:
It's all prepared now - just a matter of cooking the steak when we're ready.

ELLIE:
Oh, wonderful. Gwen, there's a letter come for you.

She hands GWEN the letter. She looks at the postmark, and, a little excited, opens it.

ELLIE:
Is it from James?

GWEN:
No. From Heather. She's the one who writes.

ELLIE:
It's always the wife who has to write the letters, isn't it?

VIV:
Yeah, and clean the toilets.

ELLIE:

What does she say - oh, I'm sorry, I don't mean to be nosey.

GWEN:

Just bits and pieces of news. Mostly about the preparations for the baby.

VIV:

Oh, she's expecting, is she?

ELLIE:

Yes, only a month or so to go now. And she's got a bit of high blood pressure.

VIV:

Oh, yeah.

GWEN:

She's getting very tired, she had to have a day in bed yesterday.

ELLIE:

Sounds like she could do with a bit of help.

GWEN:

Yes. They've already asked me if I'll go to stay for a few weeks when she has the baby, but Paul's not happy about the idea.

VIV:

So what! Do what you want.

GWEN:

That's not always possible.

VIV:

Why not?

GWEN:

I'd have thought that was obvious.

VIV:

Not to me. But then, I'm not an educated middle class woman like you. Explain it to me.

GWEN:

When you're married, you have to consider the other person.

VIV:

The husband, you mean. And does he consider you?

GWEN:

Of course.

VIV:

He doesn't bother to phone you, though, does he?

GWEN:

We have an agreement. He used to phone me, but like he said, it got silly. So I just assume he's all right, unless I hear otherwise.

ELLIE:

But doesn't he phone you just for a chat?

GWEN:

Sometimes.

VIV:

Do you phone him?

GWEN:

No.

ELLIE:

Aah, why not?

GWEN:

He, he doesn't like me to.

VIV:

Why, in case he has another woman with him?

GWEN:

No! He's often in meetings, that's all. And, and I find it offensive that you should make remarks like that. I'm very happily married.

VIV:

That's what people usually say, about six months before they get divorced.

ELLIE:

Viv! Take no notice, Gwen. Viv's not very keen on men.

VIV is becoming angry at ELLIE's behaviour

VIV:

Who says?

ELLIE:

Well, you haven't been out with anyone, have you?

(to GWEN) And usually when people get divorced they go mad, don't they - a different fella every night - but she didn't.

VIV:

Have you quite finished, speculating about me and my sex life?

ELLIE:

I'm not speculating - *(winks at GWEN)* there's nothing to speculate about.

VIV:

How do you know, stupid?

ELLIE:

(to GWEN) You've only to look at her to know that, haven't you?

VIV:

Will you bloody shut up for once, Ellie!

ELLIE sees she has gone too far, looks away from VIV and smiles awkwardly at GWEN.

A silence.

GWEN:

I thought we'd eat about 7.00. That will give us plenty of time to get ready.

VIV:

What do you mean, get ready?

ELLIE:

I told you, we're going to dress for dinner - like you do. It's all part of it, you have a bubble bath and then you do your make-up, and put on a swanky dress. Gwen's found us a dress each.

VIV:

I'll do as I am.

ELLIE:

Oh, Viv, no. You've got to dress up or you'll spoil it. I've found a gorgeous dress for you upstairs. You'll look fabulous, won't she, Gwen?

GWEN:

Yes.

ELLIE:

It's dark green velvet, full length, with this lovely frill round the neck - really glamorous. It'd really suit you.

VIV:

(sceptical) Oh, yeah.

ELLIE:

I'll get it and show you.

She hurries out.

GWEN and VIV are left alone together with nothing to say to each other.

GWEN:
She's a lovely person, Ellie.

VIV:
She's all right. She's a big baby, though, sometimes.

GWEN:
You've been friends for a long time.

VIV:
Yeah.

GWEN is still holding Heather's letter. She unfolds it a little, glances at a few words, then closes it again.

VIV:
Are you going to see them, then?

GWEN:
I'd like to.

VIV:
Don't let him stop you. Just because men get off on stopping you doing things, doesn't mean you can't go against them.

GWEN:
That's not easy, though.

VIV:

Only because the buggers frighten us. When you stop being scared you can do what you want. I learned that with Mick.

GWEN:

How?

VIV:

What?

GWEN:

How did you learn not to be afraid?

VIV:

I don't know.

She stares intently at GWEN.

VIV:

You're frightened of your husband, aren't you?

GWEN stares at her.

VIV:

(laughs) Why do we bother with them, eh? We know it doesn't work, men and women, but we keep at it.

She helps herself to a whisky, and offers to pour one for GWEN, but she shakes her head.

VIV:
Love! It achieves nothing except stories to put in the newspapers. There must be a patron saint of tabloids up there who's got a bit of influence.

GWEN:
It could be wonderful, love and everything.

VIV:
It could be, but it isn't. It's all a load of rubbish, this love and marriage stuff. I wish I'd never got married, I know that.

GWEN:
Why did you?

VIV:
I was too bloody scared to do owt else. I'd gone and got myself bloody pregnant, and I knew my Dad'd kill me if he found out, so I married Mick sharpish.

GWEN:
Oh dear.

VIV:
Oh dear? It was a bloody sight more than 'oh dear'!
It was my ticket to hell that marriage certificate.

VIV knocks back her whisky.

VIV:

I lost the baby you see.

GWEN:

Oh. I'm sorry.

VIV:

So was Mick. He reckoned I conned him into getting wed, and he spent the rest of our married life getting his revenge.

GWEN:

You could have had another child.

VIV:

Not after he'd finished knocking me about I couldn't.

GWEN stares at her in horror.

ELLIE dances into the room, carrying the dress.

ELLIE:

Sorry I've been so long. I couldn't remember which wardrobe it was in. Imagine having all those wardrobes! Look, Viv, isn't it gorgeous?

She holds out the dress. In spite of her reluctance, VIV is impressed. She has always longed to wear a dress like this but won't admit it.

VIV:

I can't wear that.

ELLIE:

Of course you can! Can't she, Gwen?

GWEN smiles.

ELLIE:

Try it on. Go on, just try it now.

VIV:

(*backing away*) No.

ELLIE pushes the dress into her hands.

ELLIE:

Feel it. Just feel how soft it is.

VIV touches the velvet gently.

ELLIE starts taking off VIV's clothes, first her cardigan and skirt.

ELLIE:

Come on. You might never get the chance of wearing a dress like this again. It's something you dream about, a dress like this.

VIV half-heartedly resists, but is obviously tempted by the dress.

VIV:

Gerroff!

ELLIE:

Hold the dress a minute, Gwen, while I get her top off.

GWEN steps forward to take the dress, and is shocked when she sees VIV unwashed and in grubby underwear.

ELLIE sees her look and is embarrassed.

A silence.

ELLIE:

Why don't you have your bubble bath before you try it on, Viv?

VIV, vulnerable and exposed, becomes aware of their scrutiny.

ELLIE:

Have you got a clean underskirt you could lend her?

GWEN:

Yes, of course.

ELLIE:

You have a lovely long soak in the bath, Viv, and then I'll come and do your hair for you. And you can try the dress on then.

VIV looks at each of them in turn and is humiliated by their dismay and their pity.

She is angry and ashamed and for a moment seems ready to strike out at them.

Then she looks at the dress, snatches it out of GWEN's hands and runs upstairs, clutching it to her breast.

SCENE THREE

VIV enters, seething and aggressive, followed by ELLIE, who is tiddly and cocky in a glitzy evening gown. ELLIE opens the drinks cabinet.

ELLIE:
Gwen said we could have whatever we want. I'm having a Cointreau - what are you having?

VIV:

(grabbing the brandy bottle) A bloody brandy!

She unscrews the top and swigs brandy out of the bottle.

ELLIE takes the bottle from her.

ELLIE:
Don't do that! You don't drink brandy like that. They've got special glasses. Look.

She pours a large measure into a brandy glass and demonstrates, inhaling elaborately before sipping delicately.

ELLIE:
That's how you do it.

VIV:
Oh, is it? You're a bloody expert now, are you?

ELLIE:

There's no need to take that tone. And I do wish you'd stop trying to put me down all the time.

VIV:

Me, trying to put you down! And what have you been doing to me all night?

ELLIE, pouring her Cointreau, ignores her

VIV:

First you put me in this bloody dress .

ELLIE:

It's a beautiful dress.

VIV:

You didn't tell me it was her mother's, though, did you?

ELLIE:

I wish Gwen hadn't let that slip out.

VIV:

A dead woman's dress. Good enough for Viv, eh? Then all through the meal you were keeping an eye on me and it was 'Not that knife, Viv,' and 'Oh, you'll have to excuse her, Gwen, she's not used to this sort of thing.'

I'm as bloody used to it as you are!

ELLIE:

I didn't want you showing yourself up, that's all.

VIV:

You made me sick tonight, do you know that!

ELLIE:

You nearly made us sick, you mean, guzzling your food like that. You did it on purpose.

VIV:

Well, I'd had enough of you acting like Lady Muck - picking at your prawn cocktail! 'These prawns are absolutely delicious, Gwen. What is the dressing? You must give me the recipe.' Pathetic!

ELLIE:

You're the one who's pathetic.

VIV:

Oh, am I! You ungrateful little bitch!

ELLIE feels a bit guilty but overcomes this with some more Cointreau.

GWEN, also wearing a long elegant dress, brings in the coffee and chocolate mints.

ELLIE rushes to make a space on the coffee table.

ELLIE:

Ooh, mints as well. Oh, the perfect end to a perfect meal.

VIV stands apart, knocking back the brandy.

GWEN sits on the sofa and pours the coffee.

ELLIE sits in the armchair facing her.

VIV watches them for a moment and then moves towards the audience - but is listening to GWEN and ELLIE.

ELLIE:

They're lovely coffee cups. Were they a wedding present?

GWEN:

Yes.

ELLIE:

And the wine glasses?

GWEN:

Yes.

VIV:

(*to the audience*)   To them that hath shall be given, eh?

(She steps further forward, displaying the dress)
And the more they get the more they want, some of them. Fantastic dress this, isn't it? Gwen's mother knew how to spend money, once she got hold of some. Vera her name was.

She was only a bit of a secretary, you know. No, she didn't marry the boss. She was too clever to do that. She married the young upstart that was smarter than the boss, the one who took over the business.
She bought this to wear at Gwen's 21st birthday party apparently.

The lights fade to focus on an area at the foot of the stairs - the size of a large hallway.

She did all right for herself, did Freda. I've nowt against that. Well, I have because she did bugger all for anybody else by the sound of it. You can imagine what sort of a mother she was to Gwen.

The lighting change is completed as VIV takes on the persona of GWEN's mother, VERA.

VIV/VERA looks at her image in a full-length mirror.

She turns away and moves across to call to GWEN upstairs.

VIV/VERA:
Gwen! Are you ready?

GWEN:
(Off stage) Yes, Mummy.

VIV/VERA:

Well, come on then - or do you want to be late for your own birthday party?

GWEN comes down the stairs, unsure of herself and unaware she is beautiful.

VIV/VERA:

(*looking in the mirror*) And will you please remember not to call me Mummy. Today, you are no longer a child.

VIV/VERA touches her hair as she preens herself a little more in the mirror, but when she turns and sees GWEN she freezes.

For a moment mother and daughter look at each other. GWEN doesn't understand but shrinks from the animosity on her mother's face.

GWEN:

Do I look all right?

VIV/VERA:

The taxi should be here in a few minutes.

GWEN:

Isn't Daddy coming for us?

VIV/VERA:

No, he phoned to say he had to meet someone.

GWEN:

Oh.

VIV/VERA:

Don't worry, he'll be at your party. And he's invited someone for you to meet.

GWEN:

Who?

VIV/VERA:

A young man. Paul Courtney. I think you'll like him.

GWEN:

Who is he?

VIV/VERA:

Do you never read the paper?

GWEN:

Yes, I read the Telegraph. Well bits of it, but it seems mostly about strikes and things at the moment.

VIV/VERA:

There are always some who don't want to work. Paul's father is the new chief executive at the building society.

GWEN:

Oh.

VIV/VERA:

It's time you thought about a life of your own, you know. A home of your own.

GWEN:

This is my home.

VIV/VERA:

Yes. You've been a very lucky girl, but you'll have to make your own way in the world sometime - just as I had to.

GWEN:

I told you, I'll get a job as soon as I finish college.

VIV/VERA:

You told me? What can *you* tell me?

GWEN looks at her.

VIV/VERA:

You're twenty-one, but we both know you aren't exactly going to set the world on fire, Gwen, don't we? *(Sees GWEN's resentful look)* Don't you look at me like that, madam!

GWEN:

Sorry.

VIV/VERA:

Your father and I realised a long time ago what your future needed to be. We just hope that you'll at least have the sense to take our advice.

GWEN:

And what's that?

VIV/VERA:

To get married of course. We can't go on looking after you for ever. And we plan to move to London before long. Just the two of us.

GWEN:

Oh.

We hear a car pull up outside the house.

VIV/VERA:

The taxi's here. Party time! Gwen, for heaven's sake, put a smile on your face!

VIV/VERA exits.

GWEN stands looking after her, and then turns to check her appearance in the mirror.

She touches her face (an echo of Act One) and then, head bowed, she exits.

VIV, back in her own persona, returns to watch GWEN exit as the lights change .

VIV:

Poor kid. But it's no excuse, and it's not as if she's gone short of anything. She had all the money her parents left her, and what did she do with it? She let her bloody husband spend most of it, with hardly any questions asked. Well, it's easier not to ask questions sometimes, isn't it? Like it's easier to switch off the tele when the news is on, easier not to think.

The lights come up on the set again.

VIV:

(*walking back towards GWEN and ELLIE*) That's what gets me about people like Gwen - they're not stupid, or mean-minded even - but they don't bloody think!

GWEN and ELLIE are still in the same places, chatting.

VIV roams around them, looking for a chance to butt in.

ELLIE:

Our Tracy had some lovely wedding presents. Gives you a good start, doesn't it?

GWEN:

Yes, people are very generous.

VIV:

Some people can afford to be. You should have seen some of the wedding presents Ellie got, talk about cheap rubbish.

ELLIE:

Only my auntie Bertha's. Our Tracy did better though, but that's what you want, isn't it, for your children to do better than you.

GWEN:

Yes.

ELLIE:

Our Tracy went to Tenerife for her honeymoon. And they'd only been married six months when they bought their own house, a lovely little terraced cottage.

VIV:

Only one bedroom, though, to make sure her Mum and Dad couldn't go to stay with them.

ELLIE:

That's a horrible thing to say!

VIV:

Have they invited you, then, now they've bought that three bed-roomed semi in Derby?

ELLIE:

No. They haven't bought it.

VIV:

I thought they had.

ELLIE:

No, it fell through.

VIV:

You didn't tell me. Where are they living now, then? You said they'd sold theirs.

ELLIE:

They have. But Tracy's got a new job. *(Looks at GWEN)* In London.

GWEN:

Oh, that sounds exciting.

ELLIE:

Yes.

VIV:

Terry won't be excited, he's just got that good job at Rolls Royce. He won't want to go to London.

ELLIE:

No.

VIV:

What's going on?

ELLIE:

(to GWEN) I've always wanted to live in London. I'll be able to go on visits once Tracy finds a flat. Do you go to London often?

GWEN:

I used to.

VIV:

Never mind that! How come Tracy's got a job in London when Terry's working in Derby?

ELLIE:

(To GWEN) Oh, of course, you like the theatre - you've got to go to London if you love the theatre.

VIV's had enough of being ignored. She grabs ELLIE.

VIV:

I'm talking to you, not her.
Tell me what's going on.

ELLIE gets up, wriggling out of VIV's grasp, and nervously goes to get another drink.

ELLIE:

You don't mind if I have another drink, do you, Gwen?

GWEN:

Of course not.

ELLIE:

You haven't got one yet, what can I get you?

GWEN:

A Bailey's please.

VIV:

Ellie!

ELLIE jumps, almost dropping the bottle. She puts it down shakily.

ELLIE:

They've split up, if you must know.

VIV looks at her friend for a long moment – it's the first time ELLIE has kept a secret from her.

VIV:

And you never told me?

ELLIE:

Why should I tell you, or anyone else for that matter?

VIV:

I'm your mate. Or I thought I was till we got here.

She turns to GWEN

VIV:

Kept this one quiet, didn't she? All through that bloody dinner, it was 'my perfect husband' and 'my perfect daughter'! And now we learn that wonderful Tracy's cocked it all up.

ELLIE:

Shut up!

VIV:

Don't you bloody tell me to shut up! Who do you think you are?

ELLIE:

(to GWEN) I don't know how it's happened. I don't understand. *(continued)*

I had it all perfect for our Tracy. I told you about the wedding and that, didn't I?

GWEN:

Yes. It sounded lovely.

ELLIE:

It was. I had something right for once. Not a cheap do, like ours was - a proper white wedding with a new dress, like in a magazine. And a proper honeymoon, and their own house. (*Ellie fumbles in her dress for a handkerchief and blows her nose*) It worked out perfect. Just like it should be. All I ever wanted. And now she's finished it. Ruined it all. Everything. No pictures to show round now. (*tries to laugh*) No glamorous grandma competitions.

ELLIE *sinks down on to a chair*

I thought I'd made it, I thought at long last, for once in my life, I'd got something right.

Close to tears, she bows her head.

VIV:

And how long has all this been going on?

GWEN:

Does it matter?

VIV:

Yes, it bloody does! For bloody years she's been throwing it at me, about how she's made a success of things - like I haven't. And it's all been a bloody con!

ELLIE:

It hasn't! It was all wonderful, it was.

VIV:

And what about Colin - what does he think about all this?

ELLIE:

He doesn't understand! He says he's sick of hearing it all. He doesn't damned well care!

VIV:

Oh, I see. Is that why he's buggered off? Had enough of you, has he?

ELLIE:

No!

VIV:

A fishing trip! I knew there was more to it than that, but you wouldn't tell me, would you?

ELLIE:

Why should I?

VIV glares at her.

VIV:

(glancing at GWEN)

Yeah. Why should you? I'm nothing to you, am I? All the years I've looked out for you, and you forget

(snaps her fingers) just like that. Do you know something?

(picking up a cushion and hurling it at ELLLIE)

You deserve what's happened, you stupid little cow!

ELLIE pushes the cushion away.

VIV moves to stand in front of ELLIE, leaning heavily over her.

VIV:

You had it all painted rosy didn't you, your little dream world. You'd got your Tracy to make it come true - only she hasn't!

GWEN:

Leave her alone.

VIV:

You shurrup!

(to ELLIE) You were a rotten mother. You brought your Tracy up to believe everything was going to be like it is in fairytales. You told her lies.

ELLIE wriggles away from under VIV's belligerence and stands facing her defiantly

ELLIE:
I didn't.

GWEN stands, afraid of VIV's anger towards ELLIE, but afraid to approach VIV.

VIV grabs ELLIE by the arm and shakes and slaps her as she speaks

VIV:
Liar! Liar! You're stupid! Do you know that! You always thought love and marriage were the answer to everything, and you conned your poor little girl into thinking the same. *(gets hold of ELLIE's hair and pulls her head back)* You weren't fit to have children, you!

GWEN takes hold of VIV and tries to pull her away

GWEN:
Leave her alone! You're hurting her!

VIV turns and shoves GWEN across the room.

VIV:
Get away you!

ELLIE has sunk to her knees, crying. VIV looks at her and is upset that she's crying.

VIV turns back to GWEN.

VIV:

I'm hurting her? It's not me that's bloody hurt her - it's you lot that's done the damage!
You've been hurting her all her life. Having what she hasn't got, and making sure she can never get it!

Kicking over the coffee table, she moves towards GWEN and begins to hit her.

VIV:

You're a taker you, like the rest of them! Well, I'll teach you to rob me!

ELLIE runs towards her screaming.

ELLIE:

No! Viv, stop it! Get off her!

VIV:

No. I'm going to have her. I'm going to show her what it's been like to be me.

She hits GWEN again

ELLIE:

Don't, Viv. Don't!

VIV ignores ELLIE, who gets to her feet and shouts louder but daren't go near VIV.

ELLIE:

Don't hit her! Don't, Viv! That's what Mick would do. Don't you be like Mick!

VIV stops, her fist still clenched in the air.

ELLIE:

You don't want to be like him, do you? Viv, let go. Let go! Please. Oh, please, Viv.

Slowly VIV lets go of GWEN and looks at her fist for a moment before backing away.

GWEN sinks down on to a chair.

ELLIE looks at VIV and then at GWEN.

She goes to GWEN and puts an arm round her.

ELLIE:

Are you all right?

ELLIE sits on the arm of the chair, holding GWEN close.

VIV looks at them.

A silence.

VIV:

I wish we'd never bloody come here.

ELLIE looks at VIV, and sees she is frightened by what has happened.

VIV glances at the telephone and then anxiously at ELLIE.

ELLIE:
You won't call the police, will you, Gwen? She didn't mean it. She didn't mean to hurt you. She's never done anything like that before.

GWEN begins to shake, clasping her hands tightly on her lap.

ELLIE:
You need a brandy. Get her a brandy, Viv.

VIV gets the drink, walks hesitantly towards GWEN and hands the brandy to ELLIE, who offers it to GWEN.

GWEN doesn't respond.

VIV picks up the overturned coffee table. ELLIE puts the glass on the table in front of GWEN and keeps her arm round her until GWEN gradually becomes calmer.

ELLIE:
We'll go.

She stands up, standing there awkwardly, looking round the room.

Then she notices the time and starts to hesitate.

ELLIE:
We'll go - first thing in the morning, Gwen. Promise. We'd go now, only it's going on for one o'clock and we'd have to get a taxi.

(*she laughs a little hysterically*) And they cost a fortune after midnight.

GWEN, recovering a little, looks at her blankly.

ELLIE gestures to VIV to leave the room.

ELLIE:
We'll go to bed, shall we? Out of your way.

Following VIV, ELLIE starts backing out of the room

ELLIE:
Do you want me to make you a cup of tea before we go up?

GWEN, still numb, shakes her head.

ELLIE:
Well, if you're all right. (*continues to move away slowly*) See you in the morning then.

She hesitates for a moment then, with VIV, exits swiftly.

GWEN stares, seeing nothing, and then she touches her bruised face.

SCENE FOUR

There are still signs of the previous night's disturbance in the room - cushions on the floor etc.

VIV stands by the window, looking out at the garden.

Her raincoat and her shopping bag are on a chair.

She turns to the audience.

VIV:

Nice out there. Me and Mick used to talk about a house with a garden. *(she pauses and looks round the room)*
We used to talk about a lot of things. I think that was what made him so mad in the end - the things we used to talk about having.

(She walks slowly towards the audience)

VIV:

He wasn't a bad looking chap. Don't get me wrong, I wouldn't have him back, no way - but it wasn't all his fault. He were a miner - but they put a stop to all that, didn't they? It wasn't just the job he lost - he lost his life, who he was. We'd no chance after that.

She stands very still, staring into space.

ELLIE enters, wearing her own clothes. She carries her raincoat folded up, and puts it next to VIV's on the chair. ELLIE stands watching VIV for a moment.

ELLIE:

Have you had any breakfast? I've just had a dish of Cornflakes. I felt a bit cheeky, helping myself after . you know, . . but I was starving. Do you want some?

VIV:

No.

ELLIE:

I'm sorry, Viv, about the way I've been with you. I got carried away with it all.

VIV:

(Shrugs) Forget it. Are we off then?

VIV picks up her coat and bag and heads for the door.

ELLIE:

Oh, I think we ought to say Cheerio. We can't just go without saying thank you.

VIV:

You what?

ELLIE:

Well, it's manners, isn't it?

GWEN enters, wearing a dressing gown.

An awkward pause.

ELLIE:

I was just saying, we wanted to say thank you before we went. It's been really kind of you, we've really enjoyed it - the food and everything. It's been like a proper little holiday, hasn't it, Viv?

VIV is staring at the bruises on GWEN's face. GWEN sees this and touches them.

VIV looks away, ashamed.

VIV:

Have you any witch hazel - the old fashioned remedy, but it does help.

ELLIE:

Is there anything we can do for you before we go?

GWEN:

I've never been hit before.

ELLIE:

Haven't you?

GWEN:

Oh, smacks from other children in the playground when I was small. My parents never touched me. But the threat was there, all the time. I knew that they wanted to hit me. It terrified me.

My husband terrifies me in the same way. He's never hit me either, but I always feel that one day he will. And so I've been living in fear of violence all my life. But now it's happened. You hit me.

VIV bows her head.

GWEN:

It's such a relief, to get it over with.

VIV and ELLIE stare at her.

GWEN:

I'm grateful in a way.

VIV:

She's cracked! Let's get the hell out of here!

ELLIE:

See what you've done! Ooh, Mick'd be proud of you!

GWEN:

I've faced the fear. Now it's gone. Thank you.

VIV:

Don't mention it. Any time!

ELLIE:

You're not mad with us then?

GWEN:

No.

ELLIE:

Oh, we can go home with a clear conscience then. That's great.

Hesitantly she moves towards GWEN

Well, I'll say goodbye then. I don't suppose we're ever likely to meet again, are we . . . unless . . .

VIV:

Come on, Ellie.

GWEN takes a hesitant step towards ELLIE and kisses her on the cheek.

ELLIE:

Are you going to be all right?

VIV:

Of course she is, don't be daft!

ELLIE:

You're not happy, are you, Gwen? (S*he takes hold of GWEN's hands)* Even though you live in a big house and have beautiful clothes. . . well, money can't buy happiness, can it?

VIV:

Oh, give over! You read too many Barbara Cartland's you!

ELLIE:

(*puts on her shabby raincoat*) It's all right for me. I can count my blessings. I know I can go back to my Colin and he'll love me - really love me. (*hugs the coat around her*) Oh, it'll be wonderful, he'll hold his arms out to me and .

VIV:

(*starting to laugh*) For God's sake, shut up!

VIV laughs and looks at GWEN who laughs as well.

ELLIE:

Oh. Sorry.
I'm going to look for a new job when I get back home, Gwen. What are you going to do?

GWEN:

Just stay here, I suppose.

VIV:

And be miserable.

GWEN looks at her. VIV has no sympathy for her.

ELLIE:

You could go and stay with your son and his wife - that was what she was hoping for in that letter, you could tell.

GWEN:

And then what - once I'd stopped being needed?

ELLIE:

Well . . It's a chance to get away.

VIV:

Her sort don't take chances. Come on, Ellie.

ELLIE opens her handbag and scribbles in a notebook.

ELLIE:

This is my address. (*tears out the sheet*) Send me a postcard if you go to Cambridge. Or write if you want to. I'll write back. I'm good at letters - my spelling's not so hot, but you won't mind, will you?

GWEN:

No.

ELLIE gives her the sheet of paper and kisses her.

GWEN:

Thank you. Take care, Ellie.

ELLIE:

And you.

VIV and ELLIE exit

GWEN stands still for a moment and then goes to wave out of the window.

Alone again she looks round the room and feels the silence.

GWEN picks up James's photograph, and holds it close.

She stares at the Edwardian lady. Almost in tears, she suddenly puts down the photograph shakily, not managing to stand it up, it falls flat on the bureau.

GWEN turns to look round the room, and then she looks at the figurine again.

She picks it up, looks at it and then hurls it to the floor - the head breaks off.

GWEN stands there in despair.

We hear a door open.

ELLIE and VIV enter. VIV has taken off her raincoat and is carrying the raincoat she originally wore. She puts it on a chair.

ELLIE:
```
We haven't any bus fare.
```

GWEN looks at them, then laughs. She opens the base of a clock and takes out her purse.

VIV:
```
Good hiding place, that.
```

She and GWEN look at each other.

ELLIE sees the broken figurine and picks up the two pieces.

ELLIE:
```
Oh, heck!
```

ELLIE holds up the headless woman in one hand. In the other she holds the head, and crooks her arm.

ELLIE:

(*sings*) With her head tucked - underneath her arm . . .

She laughs

GWEN tries to laugh too, but is nearer to tears

VIV gives her a steady look.

VIV:

You're going, aren't you?

GWEN hesitates, but doesn't flinch from VIV's gaze.

GWEN:

Yes. Yes, I think I am.

ELLIE:

To your son's, do you mean?

GWEN:

Yes.

ELLIE:

Ooh, what will your husband say?

GWEN:

He won't really care.

VIV:

Till you don't come back, and he has to explain to the neighbours that you've left him.

ELLIE:

She's not leaving him, she's just having a little break.

GWEN:

No. Viv's right, I'm not coming back - I hope.

ELLIE:

But this is your home. You can't leave all this, your china and everything.

GWEN:

That was my mother's, not mine.

VIV:

It's still worth a bob or two. You can always sell it. Don't let him rob you - make sure you get your fair share.

GWEN:

I suppose I should.

She steps hesitantly towards VIV and touches her arm.

VIV backs away a little.

GWEN:

Thank you. Do you think I'll . . .?

VIV:

Yeah, you'll be all right.

GWEN:

I hope so.

ELLIE:

I've heard it's a lovely place, Cambridge. And you never know, you might meet a nice professor or something.

VIV:

Oh, my god, Ellie, you've a one track mind you!

ELLIE laughs and gives VIV a little shove

ELLIE:

No, I haven't!

ELLIE links arms with VIV and pulls her close.

Then she looks at GWEN who tries to smile at them but is close to tears as she stands there alone and hesitant.

ELLIE drags VIV towards GWEN and puts her arm round her - drawing the three of them together.

ELLIE:

Hasn't it been nice, all girls together?

GWEN takes a handkerchief from her pocket as she gives way to tears.

ELLIE moves away from VIV and holds on to GWEN.

ELLIE:

Come on, love, I'll help you pack.

They move towards the stairs, leaving VIV behind.

VIV:

I'll wait for you here, Ellie, shall I?

ELLIE, with sudden realisation, pauses for a moment before answering.

ELLIE:

No. No, there's no need. (*then, seeing VIV's dismay*) I'll see you when I get home.

VIV:

Oh. O.K.

ELLIE guides GWEN up the stairs and they exit.

VIV watches them go, pauses, looks at the audience and walks round to pick up the cigarette lighter and the snuff box and put them in her bag.

She picks up Gwen's purse, looks in the wallet and card section but then puts it down.

She turns once more to the audience.

VIV:

I'm not taking her money or her credit cards - she'll need them. Then when her money starts running out she'll have to get a job like the rest of us - do her good. She'll open a tea room or summat.

VIV stows the silver box in her bag.

```
I suppose you don't think this is right, but
what choice have I got? (glances up the stairs)
There's no escape route for people like me.
```

She gets a bottle of whisky from the back of the drinks cabinet, puts it in her bag and closes the zip. She picks up the raincoat and puts it on. She pauses, looking back at Gwen's elegant lounge.

Seeing a cushion on the floor, she slowly walks over to pick it up and replace it on the sofa, smoothing the fabric carefully and slowly.

She stands for a moment, admiring the effect. Moving away she notices James's photograph lying flat. She picks it up and looks at it for a moment before standing it up carefully on the bureau.

She goes to the edge of the stage, pauses to look back at the lounge, then looks at the audience.

She exits abruptly.

THE END

A silence.

Then 60s music is played.

Scripts by Liz Wainwright

Does Your Mother Dance?	Stage Play
Mixed Company	Stage Play
Grounded	Stage Monologue
One in Three	TV Film
Sunshine	BBC Radio Drama
Gwyn	BBC Radio Drama
Mrs Danby's Destiny	BBC Radio Drama
A Second Summer	BBC Radio Drama
Madame	BBC Radio Drama
Somebody	BBC Radio Drama

www.lizscript.co.uk

Printed in Great Britain
by Amazon.co.uk, Ltd.,
Marston Gate.